"THE MASTER'S MIND"™

ON TOTAL SUCCESS

DISCOVER GOD'S WISDOM

FOR YOUR PERSONAL AND PROFESSIONAL SUCCESS

PRINCESS **BOLA** ADELANI

"The Master's Mind" ™ on Total Success: Discover God's Wisdom for Your Personal and Professional Success by Princess Bola Adelani

Editor(s):
Danielle Roberts
Rameika Williams- www.blessededitor.com

Cover design: Christopher Davis – http://ascensionmarketingco.com

Published by DiViNE Purpose Publishing Co., LLC
www.divinepurposepublishing.com
info@divinepurposepublishing.com

ISBN-13: 978-0692644843
ISBN-10: 0692644849
LCCN: 2016902737

Printed in the United States of America

DEDICATION

Dedicated to Jesus, my inspiration, the Love of my Life,
the Savior of the World, my Best Friend and Redeemer.

TABLE OF CONTENTS

ACKNOWLEDGEMENTS

I would like to thank my "two young lions," Emmanuel and Enoch, for their support in choosing the title of this book and for the numerous times I "disturbed their peace" to bounce ideas off them, and for offering feedback that was often wiser than their years.

To the DiViNE Purpose Publishing team, a huge thank you especially to President/CEO, LaShawn Dobbs who coached and encouraged me in the early days of writing when I was experiencing "writer's block."

To my editors, Rameika Williams and Danielle Roberts, for their expertise on the book, their prompt turn around, and for making me sound better than I really am! Many, many thanks to YOU!

Many thanks also to Christopher Davis, the Chief Design Officer at Ascension Marketing Co., for the phenomenal job on the design of the book cover.

To my close, extended, biological and spiritual family, too many to mention individually, a big thank you. I am who I am today because of my relationship with you and your input in my life.

To you, the reader, who believed in me enough to purchase and read this book, I say a big thank you.

"THE MASTER'S MIND"™

ON TOTAL SUCCESS

DISCOVER GOD'S WISDOM

FOR YOUR PERSONAL AND PROFESSIONAL SUCCESS

INTRODUCTION

"What you do not know is hurting you!" – Princess Bola Adelani

"My people are destroyed for lack of knowledge." – Hosea 4 v 6

The Bible is God's instructional manual for successful kingdom living. It is full of practical wisdom and strategies for personal and professional growth and success. The problem is that many people do not read it and those who do, often read it with religious lenses and subsequently miss the practical wisdom, liberating truth and success strategies embedded in it. This is why the Lord says in Hosea 4 v 6 that his people are *"destroyed for lack of knowledge."* In other words, what you do not know is hurting you!

In this groundbreaking and revolutionary book, I de-mystify and decode the Bible and establish from it the core hidden foundational Biblical principles for total success. I will also introduce Jesus in a more relatable way so that you can glean practical wisdom from his life and earthly ministry.

Jesus was undoubtedly one of the most totally successful and spiritual transformational leaders of all time. He was totally successful in EVERY sense of the word. He pursued his higher calling and destiny to the fullest; through his sacrificial death on the Cross of Calvary. Through that act alone, He is responsible for impacting and bringing billions of souls into God's Kingdom. ALL believers can attribute their place in the Kingdom to his efforts. There is no disputing that He transformed humanity's thinking and behavior. He passionately sought the glory of God and His life was fully aligned with His Father's will and core values. He walked in integrity, love and forgiveness and his ministry was blessed materially and financially (it had to be if He had a treasurer who was stealing from the ministry coffers, so there was obviously money to steal. He had to be affluent if the soldiers fought for his robes... He definitely was no peasant struggling to pay bills and taxes). So, in the true sense of the word, He was totally successful.

The good news is, this dynamic and totally successful Master did not leave us without the wisdom and knowledge to be as totally successful as he was. Quite the contrary, not only did he personally model and exemplify how to be totally successful, he taught us through numerous parables, sermons and messages, how to thrive and succeed God's way! We are not left without hope, and because he was, we can be also. He actually wants us not only to carry on the torch, but to do greater works than He did because He has gone to his Father (John 17).

After years of study and research, I have been able to narrow the core foundational hidden Biblical principles and factors that are responsible for total success, as taught and exemplified by Jesus, down to three! These three factors are simple, yet they are profound. Though hidden, it would be naïve to ignore their impact. I believe that if you master them, you will be totally successful and like the Bible says in James 1 verse 4, you will be "perfect and complete, lacking nothing," as you pursue your higher and eternal purpose and destiny.

The power of having a foundation cannot be over-emphasized. It is the foundation that determines the height of a thing or structure. The deeper and stronger the foundation, the higher the structure can go. Everything rises and falls on the foundation. You can ONLY go as high as your foundation.

That is why the Bible asks the profound question in Psalm 11 verse 3, *"if the foundation be destroyed, what can the righteous do?!"* The answer is that there is pretty much nothing anyone can do to salvage a situation or building with a faulty foundation. The entire structure is coming down if the foundation is damaged.

Similarly, when it comes to being TOTALLY successful at the "game of life," it is imperative that you identify and master the core foundational principles that govern and influence success - the pillars, so to speak, so that you reach as far as you desire to go in life. Your height, success, and stature will be limitless if you hone in on these three foundational principles.

Within these pages, I expose the three core hidden foundational pillars that I also refer to as the "BCC" of Total Success (because the first alphabet of each principle spells out the acronym "BCC"). BCC in computer verbiage stands for "Blind Carbon Copy," which means that the party or parties connected to and impacted by, the correspondence are hidden until revealed by the sender. Similarly, these pillars of success, though not immediately obvious to the naked eye, impact and influence our performance, productivity, and ultimately our results. It has taken the Holy Spirit years of study and research to identify them.

I am on a God-given mission to shift your mindset. To inform, inspire, motivate, and equip you to be all that God has called you to be on the earth and to be totally successful as you pursue it.

So, fasten your seat belts and get ready to soar into heights and dimensions previously unknown as I decode total success for you and REVEAL God's mind, and the three core hidden foundational principles that are responsible for total success.

Sincerely,

Your Partner in Total Success,

Princess Bola Adelani
Total Success Coach
Royal Proclamations Founder/CEO
P. O. Box 260562,
Hartford, CT 06126
(860) 967-1094
info@RoyalProclamations.com
www.RoyalProclamations.com

SECTION 1

TOTAL SUCCESS EMBRACED

CHAPTER 1

SO YOU WANT TO BE TOTALLY SUCCESSFUL?

You are in good company.... God wants you to be TOTALLY successful as well! Yes, the Creator of the universe is on your side. He desires for you to succeed in your life's purpose. He desires for everything you lay your hands upon to prosper and be successful. He desires for you to be successful in everything you do and succeed in every area of your life – totally successful- spirit, soul, body and mind! That is why He put the innate desire in you, and in every human being, for total success. It is your divine birthright. A great and powerful God wants his creation to be like him – great, powerful and totally successful.

So, welcome to the club of normal human beings! The desire for TOTAL success is one that is common to every normal human being walking the face of this earth. It doesn't matter whether they are in developing countries or undeveloped countries. Every human being desires to be successful - to succeed and prosper in everything they do and in EVERY facet of life.

Believe it or not, there was a time in my life that I struggled with my desire for success and with my calling to coach people to be totally successful, until I turned to the Word of God. I struggled because I thought God only cared for my spiritual well-being, but did not care about my emotional, material, and financial well-being. I thought that, as a Christian, it was somehow "carnal," "worldly" and ungodly of me to desire to be totally successful. The problem was with my mindset. I erroneously believed that poverty was synonymous with piety and that money, wealth, and material success were inherently evil. But when I turned to the Word of God, without the religious lenses, I saw the error of my beliefs. My erroneous belief and negative mindset was rooted in the way that I conceptualized God and that was distorted by my not so positive relationship with my biological father, and by the teachings of some of my spiritual/religious leaders. All that changed in 2012 when I began a journey of emotional healing and self-discovery. I read scriptures like Psalm 35 verse 27, which says, "God delights in the prosperity of his servants" and 1 John 3 verse 2, which says, "He desires for me to 'prosper and be in health as my soul prospers". With fresh eyes, I realized that God TRULY desires and delights in my prosperity. That is my physical, emotional, spiritual, and financial well-being.

Think about it… which normal parent would desire less than total success for his or her children? God is no different. He knows how to give good gifts to those who ask Him. He says, "If you being evil know how to give good gifts to your children, how much more will I, your heavenly Father, give you good gifts" (Matthew 7 v 11).

Actually, the truth is, God abhors anything that is unprofitable, unproductive, unfruitful and barren. We see this divine loathe for mediocrity and failure all over the scriptures. In Revelation, God spews out lukewarm people (Revelation 3 v 16), in the Parable of the Talents in Matthew 25, he casts out the unprofitable servant into darkness, and in Mark 11 v 12 -25, he curses the unfruitful fig tree. Believe it or not, God has zero tolerance for anything that isn't successful, productive, profitable, growing, flourishing, and fruitful.

God's heart and mind is so wired for abundance and total success that He commands you and I to be like him and "be fruitful and multiply" (Genesis 1 v 26-28). That is why he created EVERYTHING with the capacity to be fruitful and to multiply. God so desires for you to be totally successful that he makes a promise to you that you will not labor in vain (Isaiah 65 v 23) and ALL your labor will be profitable.

Your desire for total success is legitimate and God given.

So, my friend, it's time for you to conquer your guilt for total success. It's time for you to STOP apologizing for your legitimate, God-given desire to be successful. It's time for you to align your will with God's will and fully embrace the divine will for you to be totally successful. It's time for you to fight against anything and everything that wants to keep you average and mediocre. Your divine greatness is worth fighting for. This is what I say:

'Greatness is the ONLY thing worth fighting for, and mediocrity is the only thing worth fighting against!'

It's time for you to own your desire and intentionally and strategically go after total success. You cannot be totally successful until you conquer your guilt, fully embrace your desire, and stop apologizing for it. Any internal conflict regarding success will cause you to subconsciously self-sabotage any opportunities to be successful. The internal conflict will also slow your drive and passion for success.

Go for it! You and God are on the same side, the same team – the winning team!

Affirmation: God delights in my prosperity and my success. He desires for me to be totally successful. He desires for me to accomplish the eternal purpose for which he placed me on the planet. I conquer my fear and any form of guilt conflicting with my desire to be totally successful. Total success is my God given right and my desire is legitimate, and aligned with the Master's mind.

I fully embrace, and no longer apologize for my desire to be totally successful! I am fully present and fully engaged. I am intentional and strategic in my efforts to be totally successful.

I declare and decree that the pleasure of the Lord prospers in my hands. God teaches my hands to war and my fingers to fight. He teaches me to profit. I am profitable, fruitful, and productive in all my endeavors because in ALL labor there is profit. My profiting is apparent and obvious.

I declare and decree that I do NOT labor in vain. I will not run my race in vain. I will not bring forth for trouble. I will not lose my reward in this life and in the life to come! I will reach my goal! I will make full proof of my ministry.

SECTION 2

TOTAL SUCCESS
(RE)DEFINED

CHAPTER 2

TOTAL SUCCESS (RE) DEFINED

Success is one of those words that is very difficult to define because to a very large extent it is subjective and personal. For most people, it is the realization of a personal goal and dream.

However, in more generic or general terms, success is often defined in terms of financial and material wealth. How much money you have in your bank account, what type of car you drive, where you live, your zip code, how many houses you own, where your children go to school, and so on and so forth. While material and financial wealth is a part of being successful, TOTAL success is a little bit more comprehensive.

For me, TOTAL success, is a holistic word. It has both a spiritual and physical dimension to it. In its basic and most fundamental sense, I define TOTAL success as an intentional and strategic effort on the part of an individual to pursue God's higher purpose for their life, to their maximum ability and capacity. Note, the emphasis here is pursuing **"God's"** higher purpose and not yours!

Yes, contrary to what you may think, life is not about you! You are God's idea. Your life begins and ends with God. You are not an accident! God had something unique and very special in mind when he created you. Taking the time to discover and pursue that purpose to its fullest capacity, and accomplishing it, is what I define as TOTAL success.

I guess your next question would be; what is God's eternal purpose for me? What did God have in mind when he created me?

Good question! Let us to turn to Genesis 1 - the book that captures the story of creation, to better fathom the Master's mind for creating the human race.

According to Genesis Chapter 1 verse 26 – 28, after God created the man and the woman, he gave them a directive to **be fruitful**, to multiply, to replenish the Earth and **subdue it**. He also asked them to; *"**rule** over the fish in the sea and the birds in the sky and over every living creature that moves on the ground."* That means the tri-fold purpose for which God created humanity (you and I) is to be:

1. Fruitful, multiply and replenish the earth

2. Subdue the earth

3. Rule over it

Our role and mission on the Earth is not only to act as governors and kings over the Earth realm, making sure it operates and functions in alignment with the Master's mind and will, but we also have a responsibility to increase, advance and numerically grow the human race, biologically and spiritually.

In the spiritual sense, God wants you to reproduce after your kind. To bring forth many sons and daughters to glory. To advance his kingdom and de-populate the kingdom of darkness through the preaching and teaching of His Word. That means, your primary purpose and calling is to make disciples and bring other sons and daughters into God's Kingdom. You are to leverage ALL of the gifts, talents and resources that God has given you – as a singer, writer, teacher, speaker, cook, etc. to inspire and create change. To influence others to accept Jesus as Lord and Savior and, as a result, expand God's Kingdom here on earth.

When you are intentionally and strategically pursuing this divine purpose and mission, you are pursuing success, in its truest and purest definition. You are in alignment with God's Will. You are seeking Kingdom first. You are making it about what it truly is; the eternal destination of the souls of men. You are living on purpose and in divine alignment and being totally successful.

The mind of the Master is clear. He wants you to be fruitful, to multiply and be totally successful, FIRST and FOREMOST, in your spiritual calling, as a transformer and leader of change. He wants you to actively pursue your spiritual calling, as that is what He will reward you for in eternity.

Total success is success that is more invested in the eternal destination of humans, and not just in the accumulation of material things that are transient and will pass away. Total success is success beyond the here and now. It transcends the present world and extends into eternity.

This quest and passion for spiritual multiplication and success is clearly the heart and mind of God, because Master Jesus reiterated it in John 15 v 1-16, when he said, "We should bear fruit and our fruit should remain." This is not referring simply to fruit of the spirit, but fruit of souls.

Total success in its basic and fundamental sense is therefore about how wealthy you are, as far as how many souls you bring into the Kingdom of God! How many spiritual sons and daughters you have. How many are credited into your bank account in heaven as products of your evangelistic efforts! The MORE there are, the MORE successful you are in God's eyes and in God's definition of the word.

Many people are affluent materially and financially, but are spiritually bankrupt and barren. Spiritually, they are as poor as the proverbial church mouse. They have no fruit. They have no one that they have brought into the Kingdom. If that describes you, let me tell you right here and now that in the Master's eyes you are poor regardless of how much you money have in your bank account on Earth.

The Master measures success by how many souls you are bringing into His kingdom. You will be rewarded for your spiritual reproduction (souls won to Christ). Not by your physical reproduction (how many biological children you had) nor by how many material possessions you accumulated. The only time your biological children will count is if you witnessed to them and trained them in the way of the Lord. If your biological children do not make it to Heaven, then you have failed. If others around you do not make it to Heaven with you, then you have failed and have been totally unsuccessful in your life's mission and purpose.

The crowns and awards that will be given out in Heaven will be given based on how many souls you brought with you, not on how much you gave in tithes and offerings, or how much you sang in the choir, or how many hours you served in Sunday school! In God's economy, success, wealth and affluence are measured by souls and NOT by gold (i.e. money, cars and houses). The MORE souls credited to your heavenly bank account, the richer and more successful you are. That is why God says in Psalm 2 verse 8;

"Ask of me and I will give you the heathen for thy inheritance and the uttermost parts of the Earth for thy possession." The souls of the unbelieving men that we convert are our "inheritance" in God's Kingdom, not the amount of material wealth we accumulate.

A mindset shift is required in how we conceptualize and define success. Success according to God is not the same as success according to the world. God's prosperity and economic system runs differently from that of the world. His core values and the values of this world are totally opposite!

"What people value highly is often detestable in God's sight" (Luke 16 v 15).

The difference in the yardstick between God's and our definition of success is evident in Revelation chapters 2 and 3, where Jesus judges the seven Churches. The Church in Laodicea was judged based on their spiritual condition. Even though they were materially wealthy, in the Master's eyes they were "poor," due to their cold and lukewarm spiritual state.

Perhaps you are like the Laodicean Christian that says,

'I am rich; I have acquired wealth and do not need a thing but you do not realize that you are wretched, pitiful, poor, blind and naked." – Revelation 2:17

Just like the Master challenged the Laodicea believers to properly align their values with His, I am also challenging you to STOP "laboring after meat that perishes," but rather seek after eternal wealth and riches. STOP running after material blessings and start actively pursuing the great commission, your higher purpose and building your heavenly bank account by bringing others to Jesus! It is time for you set your affections on eternal things and lay treasures for yourself in Heaven where thieves cannot break into it and the economy NEVER crashes!

Worldly success is fleeting, temporal and can be lost in the twinkling of an eye, but total success, God's success, is permanent and eternal. Ask all those who lost money in Enron, Worldcom and in the Bernie Madoff Ponzi scheme. One minute they were rich and famous, the next they were not. That's because that was success outside of the Master's Will and plan. Success outside of God is short lived. Solomon, the richest man that ever lived, concluded that wealth that does not further God's purpose is,

"Vanity upon vanity" (Ecclesiastes 1 v 2).

Hollywood is another great example of success outside of God. They have the fame, houses, cars, etc., but many of them are miserable, and emotionally and spiritually bankrupt. They are hooked on drugs, in and out of marriages, in rehab and often die by committing suicide. That is the end of success outside of God. Only the blessing of God makes one rich and adds no sorrow with it.

I challenge you to start leveraging your gifts, talents and influence to expand the Kingdom of God. Living for a higher eternal purpose is the true definition of being TOTALLY successful.

Please do not misunderstand me. I am in no way trying to imply that there is not a financial or material dimension to being totally successful. Absolutely not. That is not my intention. Total success does include being financially and materially successful. Like I stated earlier, it is a holistic word. It means nothing missing, nothing broken. There are scriptures in the Bible that suggest that Jesus, the Master, was affluent during his earthly ministry and was NO peasant struggling to pay his bills. His financial success is evidenced by the fact that he had a treasurer (Judas) who, according to the Bible in John 12 verse 6 and John 13 verse 29, was embezzling funds from the ministry coffers. He was up to date with, and had the financial ability to pay his taxes. In Matthew 17 verses 22-27, he directed Peter to use his talent, and catch a fish that had money in it that was used to pay his taxes. According to Luke 8 verses 1-3, he had some high-level and affluent followers who supported his ministry financially and materially. So, that goes to prove that total success does include financial success.

I guess what I am trying to say is that total success or God's success is based on, and aligned with, God's Word and core values of integrity, love and forgiveness and is PRIMARILY driven by a desire to expand his kingdom on Earth. When that becomes the pursuit and ultimate goal, then the cars, houses, diamonds and everything else will be divinely and supernaturally added as needed.

God will supernaturally begin to open doors for you, give you witty ideas and inventions, and guide and lead you. He will give you wisdom, favor and boldness to be able to seize opportunities and confidently negotiate and close high figure deals and contracts. This divine ability and enablement are factors that will propel your material and financial success.

God will promote you and take you to heights and levels that are unknown to you. Ask Joseph, David, Daniel, Esther, Ruth and Jacob. These biblical characters honored God with their gift, maintained a high level of integrity and sought nothing more than to bring honor to His name and to expand His Kingdom. They will tell you that it truly pays to serve God because in the end, God rewarded and promoted them for their obedience and faithfulness with tons of material and financial blessings.

Ultimately, everything boils down to your heart, your motives, your values and priorities. When you "seek the Kingdom first," all other things will follow (Matthew 6 v 33). When you honor God, you will be like,

"A tree planted by streams of water that yields its fruit in its season, and its leaf does not wither. In all that he does, he prospers." – Psalm 1 verse 3

So, yes. Total success includes material and financial success. It is your 'WHOLE spirit, soul and body' (1 Thessalonians 5 v 23). It is success that is rooted in the spiritual – in the pursuit of your higher calling and destiny as a transformer and leader of change.

Allow God to be the source, the driving force and the reason for your success and you would have keyed into the fountain of true wisdom and power. When you align your values with His and seek success His way and for His glory, then He will bless you exceedingly, abundantly, above anything you could ask or imagine. He will bless your home, your children, your relationships and your health. He will grant you wisdom, knowledge, longevity, favor, ideas, inventions, etc. and whatever you lay your hands upon will prosper.

In conclusion, total success can be defined as Kingdom driven success. It is success that seeks first, and is focused primarily on, expanding the Kingdom of God by building relationships and influencing others for Jesus and supporting causes that do the same. It is success that is fully aligned with God's values of integrity, love and forgiveness. It abhors greed. The Bible refers to it in Joshua 1 verse 8 as "good success" (KJV).

AFFIRMATION: I am a Kingdom advancer. I am pursuing the Kingdom of God and its righteousness. As I pursue the Kingdom, God reciprocates by adding all the things I need for life and Godliness. Cars, houses, clothes, goodwill and favor are divinely and supernaturally added to me. I am intentional and being

31

fruitful in my efforts to bring others into the Kingdom of God. I am a faithful witness, boldly proclaiming the good news of the Kingdom. My values are fully aligned with that of the Master. I am not seeking wealth for the sake of it, but for the glory of God. I have my priorities in order. God blesses me abundantly and supernaturally. Money is not withheld from me because I walk uprightly. The Lord is my shepherd so I lack nothing. The heavens are open to me. I have my eyes on my eternal destination and higher purpose. The gates of hell will not prevail against me.

SECTION 3

TOTAL SUCCESS

DECODED

CHAPTER 3

THE BELIEF PRINCIPLE

"All things are possible to those that believe." – Jesus Christ (In Mark 9 verse 23)

"You shall have what you believe." - Jesus Christ (In Mark 11 verse 24)

"If you think you can or you think you can't, you're right!" – Henry Ford

Beliefs are the first hidden foundational principle that impacts total success. According to Jesus in Mark 11 verse 24, everything that you receive and achieve in this life will be directly proportional to your beliefs. This means, your beliefs govern your success and determine your results. You will only achieve and accomplish things in life for which you have the capacity to believe. No belief equals no results; little belief equals little results and much belief equals much results!

What is Belief?

"The psychological state in which an individual holds a proposition or premise to be true ... One's way of thinking and looking at things."- [Schwitzgebel, Eric (2006)

In other words, your beliefs form your mindset and your outlook on life (what you hold as true about a situation, a circumstance or about life in general). For example, if you believe people are evil, you will interact with them accordingly and your outcome in your relationship with people will be negative, because your behavior and interaction with people will be driven by your negative perceptions and beliefs. If you believe that success is unattainable then you will interact with opportunities that will make you unsuccessful and will end up with negative outcomes.

In other words, what you believe becomes your reality – a self-fulfilling prophecy of sorts! So, being totally successful totally depends on YOU. If you change your beliefs, you will change your reality. This is a great example of how much God respects the human will and mind. He gave you and me the ability to choose what we believe and be co-creators of our destinies. This also means that you are responsible for your own results and outcomes. If you believe, then you will receive, if you don't believe, then you will not receive. Each individual on the planet is the driver and architect of their own destiny and cannot blame anyone else for their failures. You are in the driver's seat. You are the boss. You are the CEO of your life.

CHAPTER 4

THE POWER OF BELIEF

The Limiting Power of Belief

According to the Master, Jesus, no one can receive anything from God without believing for it. He often said to those who approached him for blessings and healing,

'According to your faith (your belief) be it unto you!'

This means you cannot receive the supernatural blessings, favor, and goodwill from God that you need to be totally successful unless you have the belief for it. As powerful as Jesus was, his power and ability to transform lives, save souls, heal and deliver was limited by people's beliefs. In Mark 6 verse 5, the Bible says, "he could do no miracles in his hometown of Nazareth because of their unbelief."

" ⁵ And because of their unbelief, he couldn't do any miracles among them except to place his hands on a few sick people and heal them. ⁶ And he was amazed at their unbelief."

Here is Biblical proof that your beliefs are the cornerstone of your success and can have a limiting effect on how, even God, can move in your life! God cannot move in the absence of belief. God's power is LIMITED by your belief. Belief or the lack of it can be a LIMITING factor. Belief is a powerful game changer if it can impact and/or limit the power of the Almighty God!

In Mark 6 verse 5, referenced above, the people of Nazareth did not believe that Jesus was the Messiah. They did not believe He was the Son of God. They believed he was a mere mortal, an ordinary carpenter, the son of Joseph. Their lack of belief in his deity and divinity ultimately drove their behavior and attitude towards Jesus, and in turn, impacted their ability to receive from him supernaturally. Based on their beliefs, they interacted and engaged with him at the natural level, and it hindered them from receiving from him at the supernatural level.

This is how the belief system around any subject works. They act like transmitters that drive your thoughts, your words, your actions and ultimately your destiny. Beliefs deliver a direct message to the nervous system which drives behavior, attitude and choices, which in turn determines how much of our potential we harness and how much of our goals and dreams we accomplish.

The simple formula below is descriptive of how beliefs work:

Beliefs = Thoughts = Attitude = Behavior = Results

For example, if you hold certain limiting beliefs about money, you are more likely to demonstrate all or some of the behaviors listed below. These negative behaviors are all recipes for failure and will cause you to self-sabotage your financial success:

- Be tighter with money, less likely to invest, spend and give.
- Have low expectations; less likely to take risks.
- Subconsciously repel huge financial opportunities, conversations and subjects related to money
- Not negotiate for and seek opportunities for financial advancement.
- Be stressed and harbor negative emotions, negative energy that ruins relationships and performance, which closes doors to financial opportunities, and will have a huge impact on other people's willingness to help you along your journey of success.
- Lack the hope and the power to persevere, be creative and innovative.
- Lack the confidence and faith; and will be blinded to the silver lining behind the dark clouds.
- Unable to project the confidence needed for people to do business with you or hire.

The Creative Power of Belief

Beliefs are loaded with creative power. What you manifest on Earth is determined by your beliefs. *It is what creates your reality* and makes the intangible, tangible. Your belief works like a legal tender, a medium of exchange. It is the intangible "price" you tender, in exchange for all tangible material and spiritual blessings. Without it, you cannot receive ANYTHING from the "Bank of Heaven."

"For without faith it is impossible to please God... he that comes to God must BELIEVE that he is and is a rewarder of those that diligently seek him." – Hebrews 11 verse 6

There are several biblical stories that validate the fact that our beliefs are one of the major determinants of how much of God's promises we manifest. From Lazarus and Jairus' daughter who were raised from the dead, to the Syrophoenician woman's daughter that was healed, the Bible is filled with powerful stories of individuals who achieved impossible results and changed the trajectory of their lives just because they dared to believe God and take Him at His word. These amazing individuals achieved incredible breakthroughs and success, simply because they believed!

When Jesus spoke to the fig tree and it withered and died, He told his disciples that, "NOTHING is IMPOSSIBLE to those who BELIEVE." (Matthew 8 v 13, 9 v 22 & 28, 15 v 28 and Mark 10 v 52)

That means there are NO limits or boundaries to your reach and what you can achieve if you believe – (Mark 9 v 23, 11 v 23 & 24 and Matthew 17 v 20)

My favorite Biblical example of the creative power of belief in action is the story of the woman with the issue of blood, in Mark chapter five. After an encounter with Jesus, this woman became healed and changed the trajectory of her life, because she pushed past opposition and dared to believe. The kind of belief that gets results is the kind of belief that this woman had;

1. First, it had a quiet resolve and voice in her heart that believed all she needed was an encounter with Jesus.

2. Secondly, it pushed forward in the face of opposition and rejection. It persevered.

3. Thirdly, it did not take into account her past – her history and failure with other physicians, and,

4. Fourthly, it did not allow her financial situation to deter her. It had sweat equity. She was going to make it happen… somehow!

40

That, my friend, is the creative power of belief in action! Her belief created a new reality. It sent a signal to Heaven and caused her to access the dunamis (this is a Greek term meaning dynamite power) power of the Master that, upon contact, brought instant solution to a twelve year problem!

Belief says, "Yes, I can!" I can do ALL things through Christ who strengthens me. I can accomplish my goals; I can be who and what God says I am. Beliefs do not pay too much attention to facts or the economic climate. It is an inner confidence that surmounts mountains and oppositions, that perseveres in the face of trouble that says that, 'in the end I will be okay... I will win.'

What situation is confronting you? What dream do you have? What are you trying to accomplish? Be like this woman, refuse to give up. Do not let past mistakes and failures stop you. Do not allow "public opinion" and opposition, stop you. Do not allow money to stop you. Keep going forward. Keep believing. You will win if you do NOT stop. Your 'faith will make you whole.' Nothing is impossible to those who believe.

The Scientific Power of Belief

The power and impact that beliefs have on human behavior and success has been scientifically proven over the years through different tests and studies.

"What we experience is partially reality and partially what we expect to experience," says the senior letter author, Dan Ariely, a Duke University behavioral economist whose book, "Predictably Irrational," explores why people make the choices they do.

A classic example of how science supports the power of our minds and beliefs is known as: 'The Placebo Effect.' The Placebo

Effect proves that our thoughts may actually interact with the brain in a physical way.

A placebo is a fake treatment, like an inactive substance like sugar, distilled water, or saline solution. A Placebo Effect occurs when a beneficial effect, produced by a placebo drug or treatment, cannot be attributed to the properties of the placebo itself, and must therefore be due to the patient's belief in that treatment.

There are several scientific researches conducted on this subject. The most significant research in placebos have been seen in the treatment of pain. Medical researchers have found, for example, that a placebo given for pain may be as effective as 8 mg of morphine (a modest dose) [2]. Using brain scans, the University of Michigan Health System scientists found that placebo treatment triggers the brain's natural painkillers, called endorphins [3]. This study provides the first direct evidence that the brain's own pain-fighting chemicals play a role in the pain-related placebo effect – and that this response corresponds with a reduction in feelings of pain.

Another classic scientifically proven example of the power of belief in action was illustrated in 1954 by Roger Bannister's 'Four Minute Mile Run.' Prior to 1954, Medical and Sports experts said that the **human body was simply not capable of a 4-minute mile run**. It wasn't just dangerous; it was impossible. People had tried for years to break the barrier to no avail. In the 1940's, the mile record was pushed to 4:01, where it stood for nine years, as runners struggled with the idea that, just maybe, the experts had it right. Perhaps the human body had reached its limit.

However, on May 6, 1954, Roger Bannister broke the 4-minute barrier, running the distance in 3:59.4. He'd broken the world record. He'd done what so many believed was impossible. He'd made history.

Barely a year after Bannister's accomplishment, someone else ran a mile in under 4 minutes. Then some more runners did. Now, it's almost routine. Even strong high-schoolers today run 4-minute miles! After Bannister broke the barrier, the rest of the world saw that it was possible, and the previous record that had stood for nine years was broken routinely because people now BELIEVED it is possible – proving an important lesson: **once you stop believing something is impossible, it becomes possible. That is, belief drives physiological performance.**

Scientists say that our RAS is responsible for this phenomenon. The reticular activating system (RAS) in our bodies helps our brains decide what information to focus on and what to delete. When you have a clearly-defined purpose, a mission, and when you live every moment in a state of certainty that you'll achieve it, you influence what your RAS filters out and what lights it up. As a result, you pay special attention to things that help you achieve what you're after, things you otherwise would have never noticed.

The Subconscious Power of Belief

Our true beliefs are often camouflaged by positive attitude and words. Many times what we truly believe about a situation or circumstance is buried deep in our subconscious, and often not easily recognizable. The most powerful indicators about a person's beliefs are not just what they say, but what they do. As they say, actions speak louder than words.

While working with a client a while ago, she was emphatic about not having any limiting or negative beliefs around money, but the fact that she was giving her power away to her employer, and working extra hours while not earning her true worth told me another story. When I dug further, I was able to uncover her limiting belief was around her personal worth which caused her to under sell herself and not earn her true value. She did not believe in herself enough. She also believed that due to the economic recession, she needed to sacrifice her time and worth to help her employer out. This belief was limiting her financial success and earning potential. It was also affecting her performance at work and negatively impacting her relationship with her employers, because she felt unappreciated.

That is how beliefs operate. They are hidden, but drive our performance, productivity and confidence and ultimately our success. They are so concealed. it takes a masterful coach to sometimes help you to uncover them.

In the example cited above, I was able to shift the mindset and belief of this individual by making her understand that in any economy people have money for what they love and value. I said the question was not therefore about whether her employer had enough money in their budget or not, it was about whether she made them value her services enough to pay her for it. Armed with this new way of thinking, she approached her employer and was able to negotiate to stop working the extra hours she was working and not getting paid for, and actually got compensated for the hours she had been working (i.e. overtime!)

Your beliefs, whether rational or irrational, ultimately drive your attitude towards, and relationships with, money and people and ultimately impact your total success.

CHAPTER 5

THE FORMATION OF BELIEFS

There are two gateways to our soul and minds; our ear gate and our eye gate. And so our beliefs are formed from what we see and what we hear. Faith (belief), the Bible says,

"Comes by hearing and hearing by the word of God." – Romans 10 verse 17

Based on the things we are taught, especially from authoritative figures like parents, teachers, pastors, etc., we start forming beliefs about ourselves, our abilities, about people, about God and about life in general, at a very young age. The books we read, the movies we watch and who and what we listen to influence our thought processes, and form our mindset and belief system.

Also, some of our life experiences and the people around us also influence our beliefs. For example, a traumatic and abusive relationship, at a young age, may cause a limiting belief that ALL men are bad. Bankruptcy and poverty may cause someone to believe money is hard to come by, and a negative comment from a teacher can cause someone to doubt their academic competence and aptitude.

So it is important to guard your ear and eye gates, and make sure that you only listen to things that build up your faith and not tear it down. Do not allow anyone and anything to cause you to stop believing.

The method that I use to help my clients overcome any negative beliefs is to identify the root cause of that belief by going back to some of their life experiences. Once the root cause has been identified, like a skillful surgeon, I uproot it by helping them see the error of their belief and replacing it with the truth of God's word. It is very liberating because lies bind, but truth liberates.

If you are struggling with fear and procrastination, I challenge you to examine your beliefs by going over some of your life experiences from as far back as when you were a toddler. What are some of the lies people told you about yourself? What negative experiences did you have and what beliefs did you form around those experiences? Take a close look today, and review your beliefs in light of God's word. Do they line up with the word of God? If not, uproot them and allow the truth of God's word to set you free!

John 8: 32;

"You shall know the truth and the truth shall set you free."

CHAPTER 6

THE FIVE ESSENTIAL BELIEFS FOR TOTAL SUCCESS

To be totally successful, you must hold five fundamental beliefs. They are:

Believe in God: You have to believe in the supernatural power of God to succeed. There is more to making money and being successful than meets the eye. There is a spiritual dimension to financial or any type of success. Human power is limited but God's power is unlimited. When you believe in God you are able to access a limitless fount of inspiration, wisdom, goodness and mercy that will propel you forward in life.

Believe in Yourself: Life's failures and challenges has caused many to lose faith and confidence in themselves, but without belief in yourself, you cannot succeed in any type of endeavor.

Believing in yourself is not the same as being cocky or boastful, or thinking that you know it all. Rather it is a quiet, inner confidence that believes that you cannot fail. A mindset that does not take failure personally, but rather views failure as a Much Better Alternative ("M.B.A.") from the school of Life – seeing mistakes and failures as learning a **M**uch **B**etter **A**lternative…. a way of not doing what you just did. Someone once said, "Failure is success, if a lesson is learned from it."

They once asked Thomas Edison who failed a thousand times before his breakthrough discovery of the lightbulb why he did not give up after each failed attempt. His response was that he viewed each failed attempt as a way of not doing it. Wow! This is the attitude I am talking about. A winner's attitude.

There are no limits to what you can achieve on Earth. The only limits are the ones that exist in your mind. Your race, gender, educational background, socio-economic status, age, physiology, economy, country of residence, are NOT enough to limit you from achieving your God-given goals and dreams. So, I challenge you to regain the trust and confidence in yourself. Recapture that belief in who you are and what you are capable of doing.

Believe in Your Abilities: Many of us have been called names that negatively affect us and speak against our abilities. Names like "fat," "stupid" and "incompetent" can have a negative impact on how you see yourself. But nothing can be furthest from the truth. Everyone on the planet has a God-given talent and ability. You just need to discover yours, hone it and stay in your lane. You have to believe not only in yourself, but in your abilities. Believe you have what it takes to be what God has called you to be. You have the talent, skills, wisdom, strength and power to be all that you are called to be, and to achieve all your God-given goals and dreams. You were made in the image and after the likeness of God. Psalm 139 verse 14 says, 'You are fearfully and wonderfully made.' And trust me, God does not make trash! You have been specially crafted, equipped and packaged by the Master Craftsman himself. So, believe in your abilities. Stop believing the lies about who you are that have been spoken over your life by people.

Believe in People: People govern this planet and any kind of success and goodwill you will experience in this life will come through people. You have to believe in people to succeed personally and professionally. Believe in the goodness of people. Many individuals allow negative experiences that they've had with a few people cause them to have negative beliefs and attitudes about people in general. They get bitter. They have a "chip on their shoulder' and wonder why all their relationships end up badly, and why they are constantly failing. They think they are jinxed. But it is not that they are jinxed, it is just that they are filtering their relationships through negative experiences, pain and brokenness. This causes them to make poor choices, develop negative attitudes, and become angry and defensive. All this negativity is what causes them to struggle in their relationships because, for the most part, our interactions are heavily flavored by what we bring to them. Believe the best of people. When people know you expect the worst of them, they will usually act according to those expectations. When you expect the best of people, and they're aware of it, they'll generally do what they can to live up to those expectations.

Of course, some people will never like you and will disappoint no matter what you believe about them but generally speaking, most people are not out to get you; believe that they are there to support you. When you believe in people and start relating to people from a place of positivity all the goodness will come back to you a hundredfold.

Believe in Possibilities: Have you ever met people who had a million and one reasons why something is not going to work? Why your dream and vision isn't feasible? They are the worst kind of people to have on your team. They criticize everything, point out all the things that are wrong and who did something similar and failed! I am sure you know of a few people like that! Have you also noticed that these people are also stagnant in life? They are usually in the same place for years. That is the effect of having unbelief. It cripples you. It will not allow you to venture out, to try out and to take risks… all traits needed to be totally successful. Believe in possibilities. Take risks, venture out. I agree with the popular adage that says, "Nothing ventured, nothing gained." You have nothing to lose and so much to gain. Jesus said, ALL things are possible to them that believe… yes, impossible really means I'm – Possible!

So, here it is in a nutshell. You need the belief G.Y.A.P.P. to be totally successful. Here is what I mean by G.Y.A.P.P. Believe in God. Believe in Yourself. Believe in your Abilities. Believe in People. Believe in Possibilities... Don't stop believing! That is the winning formula and mindset for total success.

CHAPTER 7

'R. A.V.E.' ™

TO MASTER YOUR BELIEF

Hope isn't lost. No matter how old you are, it is still possible for you to master your beliefs, reprogram your mind and change your thinking. It is still possible to align your mind with God's mind and have the mindset of champions and winners, which believes and says, "I can do ALL things through Christ who strengthens me" (Philippians 2 verse 13). It is still possible for you to uncover and get rid of the limiting beliefs that are buried in your subconscious and are keeping you bound to mediocrity. It is still possible to take every negative thought captive and bring it to the obedience of Christ.

I am sure by now your question is how... how do I, according to Romans 12 verse 1 and 2, RENEW my mind and bring it in alignment with the will and mind of God? The answer is through my 'R.A.V.E.'™ Technique! Yes, you RAVE about yourself and to yourself at least three times a day and before long, the result is a renewed, confident, faith filled mind that is positioned for total success. Now, let me break down the four power-steps involved in the R.A.V.E. re-programming technique.

STEP 1: Rebuke your Fear: The first step in mastering your beliefs and reprogramming your mind is for you to identify your fear, confront and REBUKE it. The opposite of belief is fear. That means when belief is absent, there is some type of doubt, mistrust and fear lurking around. It may be a fear of failure, financial hardship, ridicule, rejection, loneliness or even the fear of success. Yes, some people are afraid that success may cause them to lose their humility or salvation, and are secretly afraid of success. Subconsciously, they do not believe that God can keep them on the mountain top, as well as in the valley.

You rebuke your fear by exercising your God-given authority in Matthew chapter 18 verse 18, which says, "Whatever you bind on earth is bound in heaven." When you bind the spirit of fear, doubt and unbelief, you pull down that stronghold and you are now commanding that spirit to let go of your mind. God has not given you the spirit of fear, but of power, love and a sound mind.

STEP 2: Affirmations: The next step to mastering your belief after you have identified your fear and rebuked it is for you to affirm and speak God's Word over your life. Remember, faith (belief) comes by hearing and hearing by the word of God. There is no one more powerful than you to speak faith filled words to you. Start affirming positively your goals and dreams, who you are and what you are going to achieve. Start declaring and affirming that total success is your portion. Declare that whatsoever you lay your hands upon will prosper. Affirm that you are a kingdom seeker and God adds every good gift to you.

Affirmations work by reinforcing truths into our subconscious and getting rid of the lies that we have believed. Even the master, Jesus, made very many positive statements about himself. In Luke chapter 4, he declared that the spirit of the Lord was upon him, in John 16: 6, he declared that he was the way, the truth and the life. In John 10 verse 11, he declared he was the good shepherd and in verse 9, he says he was the gate, the door to eternal life. If the Master was not bashful about declaring and affirming who he was and what his mission was, you do not need to be embarrassed about doing the same. Declare that you are blessed, and you are the head and not the tail, above and not beneath. Declare that you are an overcomer, more than a conqueror. Declare that God has given you all things that pertain to life and Godliness. Affirm that you are beautiful, created in God's image and beloved. Affirm that you are the apple of God's eye, and you are God's anointed. Affirm that angels are your bodyguard and no evil befalls you. Affirm your divine royalty and priesthood... that you are called, chosen and the beloved of God.

And like Author and motivational speaker, Jim Rohn says, "when you start thinking and saying what you really want, then your mind automatically shifts and pulls you in that direction," and like the Master Jesus says. "You will have what you say!"

The power of life and death is in your tongue. Speak life over your life and the negative depressing thoughts that limit your success will flee! That is why after each chapter I have provided some short affirmations that you can memorize. Memorize the ten truths about money provided at the end of this chapter, and affirm them daily for a prosperous and positive money mindset.

The Master says in Mark 11: 23 that we are able to change our physical circumstances through our words. Speak to your mountain of defeat, failure and fear. Command it to be removed and cast into the sea and it will obey you. Your words have power.

STEP 3: **V**isualization: The third step in mastering your belief and reprogramming and aligning your mind and thinking is for you to regularly visualize where you are trying to go. Visualization according to Norman Vincent Peale is to "formulate and stamp indelibly on your mind a mental picture of yourself being successful. Hold this picture tenaciously. Never permit it to fade. Your mind will seek to develop the picture." That means you create a mental picture of wealth, abundance, and success.

Many people think that the practice of visualization is somehow ungodly or unbiblical. Nothing could be farthest from the truth. God encouraged Abraham to visualize his greatness and his dream by asking him to go and count the stars in Genesis 15 verse 5 and as far as his eyes could "see" in Genesis 13 verse 14: so will be the expanse of the land for Abraham and his promised seed. After the visualization exercise, the Bibles says in Genesis chapter 15:1 that Abraham BELIEVED in the Lord. Connecting his faith with a visual picture… with tangible elements and things he could see naturally helped to strengthen his belief and faith in the Lord. That is the power of visualization. That is how it works. Pictures, they say, speak a thousand words. There is something about getting a picture in your mind and connecting a picture to your dream that brings it alive, makes it real and more achievable.

5 And He took him outside and said, "Now look toward the heavens, and count the stars, if you are able to count them." And He said to him, "So shall your descendants' be." 6 Then he believed in the LORD and He reckoned it to him as righteousness." – Genesis 15 verse 5 & 6

Joseph, was another Biblical example of someone God helped to visualize his dream by giving him a vision of the sun, moon, and eleven stars bowing down to him...

"Soon Joseph had another dream, and again he told his brothers about it. Listen, I have had another dream, he said. "The sun, moon, and eleven stars bowed low before me!" – *Genesis 37 verse 9 (New Living Translation)*

This visual vision helped to strengthen Joseph's belief. He would never let go, nor compromise on his dream. He probably had this vision indelibly embedded in his mind when he told the Butler years later to remember him when he got out of jail. He knew the prison was not his final destination. He knew without a shadow of a doubt where he was going because he had "seen" it years prior when God gave him the vision. This is how powerful having a visual picture of your destination can be. It buries your vision (your plan) deeply into your subconscious, then it helps you to create an inner picture of your destination and serves as a propellant and activator that drives you to attract and create it.

The Bible says in Habakkuk 2 v 6 that you should write the vision... draw the vision and make it plain. Make it visually understandable, legible and easy to read. This is why creating a vision board is so important.

"The LORD answered me: Write down this vision. Clearly inscribe it on tablets so one may easily read it" – Habakkuk 2 verse 6 (Holman Christian Standard Bible).

Create a vision board of TOTAL success. That is a board of your prospering spirit, soul and body – Put your relationship with God first, family second and career third. Visualize your wealth and abundance – find images that bring your goals and dreams alive, paste them on the board and place the board where you can see it every day and before long, you will soon attract what you "see" into reality.

STEP 4. Enclose: The fourth step of the RAVE technique to master your belief and have a positive can-do mindset is to Enclose. Enclosure is an intentional act on your part to permanently eradicate from your space ANYTHING that is negative. You tune out negativity by enclosing your eye and ear gate. This means being very selective and careful about what you watch, read and listen to. Being selective about what you allow through your eye and ear gates. Enclosure also means being selective about who is in your inner circle. Belief and positivity are contagious, but so is fear and negativity. If you hang around people who are "unbelievers," trust me, their unbelief will rub off on you and you will not have the right mindset for total success. The bible says you should guard your heart with all diligence, for out of it flows the issues of life.

"Guard your heart above all else, for it determines the course of your life." – Proverbs 4 verse 23 (New Living Translation)

In other words, we are admonished to be mindful about what we allow into our spirits and into our minds. Be careful of who you allow to speak over you. You must feed your faith and starve your fears.

Listening to negative sensationalized news, constantly bombarding and filling your mind with negative reports only serve to feed your doubts and your fears. Make a list of at least three negative things you are going to eliminate from your life over the next couple of weeks, and three positive things you are going to add, for example, motivational messages, seminars, etc.

Another important thing to eliminate is negative words. When you speak negative words, you release negative energy, death and defeat not life and power. Make sure your words line up with your faith. Phrases like; "I can't, it is impossible, I can't afford it, it is too expensive, it can NEVER happen, it's over, I am finished, it's incurable," and so on, must be eliminated from your vocabulary. For example, instead of saying, "I can't afford it." You could say, "I am not willing to invest in that purchase at this time." Remember, you can do all things through Christ who strengthens you, and ALL things are possible to those who believe.

In conclusion, when all is said and done, the most powerful way to conquer your fear and master your belief is to do what Nike says, "Just do it!" Take calculated risks! Step out in faith. Feel the fear and do it anyway. *"Believe and act as if it were impossible to fail,"* says Charles F. Kettering. Your action steps are the greatest and fastest way of building your confidence and mastering your belief. Faith without works, according to James chapter 2: 15, is dead. You will not strengthen your faith muscles if you never exercise them. Set what you believe afloat, go after your dream and God-given destiny, and do not be afraid of failure. After all, like I stated earlier, failure is only your "M.B.A." (**M**uch **B**etter **A**lternative) from the school of life. It doesn't define you. It only means that you learned a Much Better Alternative. Keep on going, put failure in perspective, and don't take failure personally; don't allow it to define you. Keep pressing. You will win if you don't quit. Keep on believing and keep on keeping on!

AFFIRMATION: Declare this truth about Money to **attract** wealth, reprogram your mind and shift into an **abundance mindset:**

- Money hasn't left the planet
- Money NEVER leaves
- Money is Fluid
- Money ONLY shifts location
- There is an abundance of "fish" (Money) in the sea
- The problem is NEVER with the "fish" (Money)
- The problem can only be with the fisherman, woman and/or net
- Money can be attracted
- Money can be followed
- Prosperity is possible in ANY economy.

CHAPTER 8

THE CONNECTION PRINCIPLE

"Abide in Me, and I will abide in you. A branch cannot bear fruit if it is disconnected from the vine, and neither will you if you are not connected to Me..." – John 15 verse 4 (The Voice)

"Don't be fooled... bad company corrupts good character." – 1 Corinthians 15 verse 33 (NLT)

"Show me your friends and I will tell you where you are going or not going!" – **Princess Bola Adelani**

The second hidden foundational principle that impacts your work-life success is the connection principle.

What is a Connection?

Connections speak to the link to which a relationship, a person, thing, or idea is associated with something else. In this case, it is about the connection between people and success. Connections

59

determine the flow of energy from one individual to another or one thing to another, and as a result a huge determinant of success because we all operate on energy. As people who are in constant motion, we cannot get from one point to another without energy... without power.

Since Connections determine how much power is flowing into an individual and how much power or energy is emanating from that individual to others, it means that our connections ultimately impact our mobility - how far we will reach in life.

There are three main factors that connections impact. They are:

1. Your Power - The amount of power you wield

2. Your Reach - The extent of your reach

3. Your Influence - The depth of your Influence

I will illustrate each factor by using three very common analogies in the next chapter.

CHAPTER 9

THE POWER OF CONNECTION

Your Connection and Your Power

Think of an electric output, the flow of energy to the equipment depends on the CONNECTION of the output to the power source. If the connection is deep and secure, then power will flow and the equipment will function at maximum capacity. If the connection is shallow or loose, the power flowing to the equipment will be insufficient to get it to operate at all, much less operating at maximum capacity.

That is exactly how connections work for us as humans. How much power you generate to function at maximum potential is dependent upon the quality and depth of your connections.

No Connection = No Power

Poor Connection = Low-Power
Deep Connections = High-Power

If you are not functioning at and maximizing your fullest potential, check your connections. How solid and deep are they? Who are they with? Are you connected with influential and powerful people?

Your Connection and Your Reach

The second factor that your Connections impact is your reach. Have you ever been on the phone and got to a location where you lost CONNECTION or have you ever tried to reach someone in a country where your telephone carrier has no connection? What happens? You cannot reach someone where your telephone company has no connection. It is virtually impossible to reach anyone where there is no connection. Connection means access, it means reach!

That is how connections impact reach. Your geographical reach and ability to reach people in different locations and at a higher level is determined by your connection. You have to have connections in the place, location, arena and level that you are trying to reach. No Connection = NO reach.

No Connection No Reach

For you to be totally successful, in all areas of your life, you have to have a broad network across all kinds of lines so that you are able to reach a broad spectrum of people with products and services. Whether you are in ministry, business or a career professional, your reach is going to be determined by your connections. Life is all about people. We are all in the people business. The larger and broader your connections, the more people you can reach with products and services. The higher the level of your connections, the further up and faster you can climb the corporate ladder and reach your corporate goals and dreams. Having a connection where you are trying to go, means you have someone that can speak for you, recommend, advocate, refer you and can open the door for you. It means access. Without that vital connection, you lack the ability and credibility to get there.

Jesus was one of the most ethnically and socio-economically diverse and connected transformational leaders of all time. His connections extended beyond his hometown of Nazareth. He was always on the go, interacting with scribes, Pharisees, tax collectors, and sinners. He travelled from Judea to Samaria and everywhere in between. He had connections in high and low places, among the downtrodden and among the rich and famous. From Nicodemus who came to him by night, or Joseph of Aritmatheau who gave his tomb for his burial, the Master was definitely a mover and shaker and very well connected at different levels! To be totally successful, you have to step outside of your comfort zone and be intentional about building relationships outside your geographical area and community, outside the four walls of your church and outside your social class and ethnicity.

If you are not 'moving and shaking' and not 'upwardly mobile,' check your connections! Are they with high-caliber people? Are your connections with influencers and decision makers? People I call, "gate-keepers?" People who can give you access to "eat at the King's table." You won't be great if those in your circle aren't great. Eagles flock with eagles. You will only get as far as you are connected.

The advent of social media and internet has turned the world into a global village, and made it possible for us to build connections internationally. I am living proof of the powerful role social media plays in helping to establish and build large and global networks. I am a huge advocate for having a recognizable and credible social presence.

It never ceases to amaze me how many people still haven't got with the social media program yet. Some are not present, some are hardly present and some do not even take their presence seriously! They have shoddy photographs, post inappropriate material and generally lack proper social etiquette and decorum. If that describes you, you are hurting your career big time. The first place people go to check you out is on the internet and one of the first few pages that show up on the search engine are your social pages. Make sure they represent you well.

Also, a lot of influencers and decision makers, that are often unreachable in person, are quite reachable socially. LinkedIn, Facebook, Twitter and Instagram are some of the popular social media websites that allow you to connect personally with others. Connecting with people socially is a good way of expanding your network and a good leverage to grow personally and professionally. Many people I know found their dream job through a posting on social media and many others have found their life partners through the same platform. So, it's not only valuable professionally, it is valuable personally. Do not overlook the power of social media and the internet as you seek to broaden your reach and actualize your God-given goals and dreams.

Your Connection and Your Influence

The third factor that our connection impacts is our influence. There is no way you can influence people that you have no connection to and vice-versa. The more connected you are with people, the more things you have in common with them, the deeper your relationship and association, the greater your ability to influence them.

There is a popular business adage that says, "People do business with those they know, like and trust." The more people that connect with you, the more they will feel like they KNOW you and the more people feel that they know you, the more people will like and trust you and do business with you! Doors will open for you as a result. Your ability to influence people to hire you for a position, invest in your dream or business and/or buy a product or service will be enhanced. It will also mean that you have more people in your corner that can influence others to do so. This ultimately translates to success financially, professionally and spiritually - More souls are credited into your heavenly account as you influence people for Jesus, and more dollars and cents credited into your earthly accounts as you influence people to buy your products and services and into your mission. That is TOTAL success in the true sense of the word!

NO Connection NO Influence

The Master was a classic example of someone who connected well with people at every level. He met people where they were. He was relatable, accessible and authentic. He "hung-out" with sinners, dressed liked the people, so much so they could not single him out from his disciples when they came to arrest him. He was one of the guys. He sat where they sat, ate what they ate, and wore what they wore. He connected with them by speaking to them in a way that they could understand. He used parables, analogies and stories that connected people with his message. All of this contributed to people feeling like they knew him, and I believe, was one of the key factors responsible for his total success.

Paul put it like this in 1 Corinthians 9: 20,

"To the Jews I became like a Jew, to win the Jews. To those under the law I became like one under the law (though I myself am not under the law), so as to win those under the law."

Rather than focusing on your disagreements, make an effort to find common ground and mutual interests whether based on gender, age, race, faith, socio-economic status, profession, etc., with others. You will discover that there is more that unites us than divides us. As you focus on what connects you with people instead of what divides you, you will find that people will find you relatable, and will better connect with you and your message. It then becomes easier for them to buy into whatever it is you are selling.

Another powerful way to grow professionally is to seek out and join professional associations and other natural groups who share in your interests. In those associations, the point of connection and mutuality is already established. There is a shared bond and mutual interest that fosters trust, unity and solidarity, which makes influence easier to accomplish.

A note of caution though; establishing connection with people is not just a physical or natural thing, it is also spiritual and intuitive. The Bible says in Psalm 42: 7: *"deep calls unto deep"* and in 2 Corinthians 5: 16, "know we no man after the flesh." In other words, we don't just know people naturally and physically, but we discern them spiritually. So, as you seek to build powerful and profitable relationships and alliances, don't just rely on your five senses!

A classic Biblical example of a connection that, I believe, was spiritually discerned, is that between Ruth and Naomi. I believe that Ruth intuitively knew that Naomi was somehow connected to her destiny, and that her connection with her would propel her towards it. As a result, she stayed connected with Naomi at a time when, in the natural, Naomi had NOTHING good going for her and NOTHING good to offer Ruth. Ruth refused to let go of Naomi long after her sister in law had gone back to what was familiar. Orpah disconnected with Ruth and fades into oblivion. We never hear of her again. Naomi stays connected and enters into greatness and has her name become engraved and immortalized in the pages of scripture.

Allow God to prayerfully lead you. Don't base your decision on outward appearances only. Things aren't always what they appear to be. Ask Samuel, he almost missed ordaining the next king of Israel because he was focused on outward appearances and qualifications, or ask King Saul who would have lost a war to the Philistine's Goliath, because he nearly wrote David off as a little kid.

As you have seen, much of your success rises and falls on your connections and as such, you cannot afford to be complacent or nonchalant about it. Don't minimize the power of connections. Get intentional about building profitable connections, TODAY!

CHAPTER 10

THE THREE ESSENTIAL TYPES OF CONNECTIONS

For you to be totally successful at work and in life, there are three essential types of connections that you absolutely have to make. These three types of connections must be congruently aligned for all aspects of your life to be in sync, harmony and balance. They are:

1. Your upward spiritual connection with God,
2. Your inward connection with your passion and purpose, and
3. Your outward connection with others

We are now to going to critically examine each of these types of connections, and discover how they impact your total success.

Upward Connection

Your upward connection speaks to your relationship with God. It is about how deeply connected you are to Jesus, the head of the body and the head of the unseen supernatural world. This connection is vertically shaped and is foundational in nature, because it is this connection that determines the quality of the two other types of connections. Actually, the other two types of connections take their shape from this one. This is because Jesus is the source from which life flows and it is from him that the whole of creation derives their existence.

"For in him we live and move and have our being.' As some of your own poets have said, 'We are his offspring." – Acts 17 verse 28 (New International Version)

Without the breath of Christ in us, we lack life, energy and power – we are lifeless. It took God breathing into the lifeless body of Adam for him to become a living soul. God is not just the source of life, he is life personified.

"Then the LORD God formed a man from the dust of the ground and breathed into his nostrils the breath of life, and the man became a living being" – Genesis 2 verse 7.

When your vertical connection is straight and upright, then your inward connection with your purpose, passion and calling, and your outward horizontal connection with others, will form a right angle and will be congruently aligned. The better aligned an individual is with God, who is the head of the body, the better aligned that individual will be with others, and the higher their chances of being totally successful. Anything outside of that geometrical formula becomes chaotic, problematic and out of order. This explains why many of our professional and personal relationships are falling apart. People are trying to build relationships with one another without their relationship with God! The equation is simple:

Successful Relationship with God = Successful Relationship with Self = Successful Relationship with People.

Jesus is the vine and we are the branches and for us to be fruitful, productive and prosperous, we have to be deeply connected to him because all the "nourishment" we need to thrive and prosper is derived from him. Without him, we can do nothing. Jesus said in John 15:4,

"Abide in me, and I will abide in you. A branch cannot bear fruit if it is disconnected from the vine, and neither will you if you are not connected to me."

To be well connected with Christ is tantamount to being connected to:

The Head of the Body

"Christ is also the head of the church, which is his body. He is the beginning, supreme over all who rise from the dead. So he is first in everything." Colossians 1: 18

The head is the organ that houses the brain. And it is from the brain that oxygen flows to other parts of the body. It is also from the brain that the nervous system receives the messages that direct the function of the other parts of the body. That means to be deeply connected with Christ is to be connected to an endless supply of 'oxygen' that you need for survival. It also means to be connected to an endless supply of inspiration, wisdom and ideas that you need to function and thrive. As the body cannot function

71

effectively without the head, similarly, we cannot function at full capacity without our connection with Christ.

The Source of Life

"All things came into being through Him, and apart from Him nothing came into being that has come into being." – John 1:3

Christ is the source of life and ALL energy. He is to us what a generator plant is to electricity. Without the generator, electricity lacks the power and ability to give light. Without a deep and strong connection with Jesus, you lack the ability to function and shine your light and brilliance. The brighter you can shine and walk in your brilliance, the more successful you will be at work and in life. Being vertically connected with Christ therefore, means you will have the power and ability to shine your light to its maximum potential and that, in turn, positions you for total success because, according to Isaiah 60:3, "kings will be drawn to the brightness of your rising!"

The Owner

"The earth is the LORD's, and everything in it. The world and all its people belong to him." – Psalm 24:1

Imagine being well connected with the owner of your company! Imagine the connections, privileges and influence that you would have access to! That is exactly what it is like to be well connected with Jesus. It means you will have access to everything and everyone he owns and that is EVERYTHING and EVERYONE. Wow! It means you will be very powerful and influential. Get in right standing with the Master, today, and position yourself for total success.

The Ruler

"And from Jesus Christ, He is the faithful witness to these things, the first to rise from the dead, and the ruler of all the kings of the world. All glory to him..." – Revelations 1: 5

Jesus is not only the owner; He is also the ruler of all the earth. He is the supreme and final authority over the affairs of this earth. He is the "governor among the nations" (Psalm 22: 28) – the sovereign ruler that reigns supreme. The buck ends with Him. His government is eternal. He was not voted into power, so He cannot be voted out of power, nor can He be impeached. When He says yes, nobody can say no. When He says no, nobody can say yes. His power and authority cannot be challenged or questioned. When He blesses, no one can curse, and when He curses, no one can bless. He kills and He makes alive. He is God all by himself. He does not need permission to be God. As the ruler, we are all his subjects and we are all under his authority. Hallelujah!

Being in right standing and connection with Him therefore means that you are backed up by the supreme, and final authority over the earth and heavenly realm. It means that you are in favor with Him and you are protected and secure. It also means that no one can question or challenge any blessings and favor that He bestows on you. It means walking in limitless power and authority. It also means that you are globally connected and have access to a global network of people who are His subjects.

Outward Connection

The second type of connection essential to your total success is your outward connection. That is to say, your connection to people. Success is not solitary. It is a collection and network of relationships because no one of us self-exists. The only person that self-exists is God, and hello, you're not God! We are all social beings that are inter-dependent on each other for survival. You need me and I need you. Being in proper and healthy connection with people will determine what you give and what you receive, which will ultimately drive your success.

Your Outward Connection will determine the following five factors that are critical to your personal, professional and financial success:

Your Magnificence

Imagine the world as this big jigsaw puzzle. Each piece of the jigsaw is unique and can stand on its own, but the beauty and true value of each individual piece cannot be fully appreciated until it is connected to the other pieces. That is exactly how our outward connections work. We are all a unique piece of the whole, but it is only when properly connected to the other pieces that our true magnificence and value can be seen and fully appreciated. The more properly aligned and connected you are with the other pieces, the better your beauty and glory will manifest. The extent of your manifested glory and splendor rises and falls on your connections. The more magnificence you manifest, the higher your value and worth, and the higher the income you can command.

This is why it is pivotal that you master how to network to make the right kind of connections. The wrong kind of connections can be catastrophic. In the jigsaw puzzle analogy described above, it is disastrous for a piece when it is not properly connected. That piece looks uncomfortable and out of place. This is how it is when you are not properly connected. You feel out of place, disjointed, and awkward. When you release those bad connections, you drive those toxic people away from you.

Your Talent Pool

Since you are not the omniscient and all sufficient God, it means that you do not possess the entire skill set and expertise required for you to actualize your goals and dreams. Someone else has the talent and skill set that you require to propel you to the next level. So, the more of the right kind of people you are connected to, the larger the pool of talent that you can draw from to actualize your goals and dreams and be totally successful. Each individual on the planet brings something valuable to the table. We are a TEAM and; "**T**ogether **E**veryone **A**chieves **M**ore!" Romans 12: 4-6 captures it succinctly.

"For just as we have many members in one body and all the members do not have the same function, 5 so we, who are many, are one body in Christ, and individually members one of another. 6 Since we have gifts that differ according to the grace given to us, each of us is to exercise them accordingly..."

Your Leads

No matter how brilliant you are, you need the good will, referral, recommendation, patronage, vote, etc. of others to propel you forward towards your goals and dreams. Your outward and horizontal connections are crucial to your total success because you need the opportunity that someone will afford you, so that you can fulfill your life's mission and purpose. I always say, "You are only five people away from your goals and dreams!" Someone knows someone, who knows someone, who knows someone, who knows someone, who can help actualize your God-given goals.

75

Your Harmony

If you are constantly feeling drained, tired and unable to function, check your connections. Who are the people in your immediate sphere of influence? Are they "parasites," negative, "dream killers?" Are they headed in the same direction as you, or are you in constant conflict, constantly trying to justify yourself and your vision? If that is the case, it is time for you to let them go and seek out the right type of connections. Seek out like-minded people, visionaries, dreamers, and people who would infuse you with positive energy, courage and inspiration. This is what I say to my clients all the time;

"Show me your friends and I will tell you where you are going or not going!"

Your connections are either propelling you with their positivity or immobilizing you with their negativity. Someone once said, "You are a reflection of the five closest people to you." 1 Corinthians chapter 15 verse 33 puts it succinctly when it says,

"Be not deceived, evil companions' corrupt good manners."

Your Opportunities

When you have the right connections you are privy to a lot of information and opportunities before they ever become public. You also have someone speaking for you in the corridors of power. You have someone advocating for you. You have someone opening doors for you. People are bridges. It is not always about your credentials and about how brilliant you are, that is a given. Most of your competitors are equally as brilliant. When it comes to the nitty gritty, it boils down to who you know and who knows you. Get out of the cubicle mindset and start networking and socializing with the "who's-who" in your industry, and watch yourself begin to accelerate professionally and actualize your dreams.

There is a mindset that is prevalent, especially among Christians, that makes them resistant to the idea of networking. They claim to be, "trusting in God for their blessings." They have this fatalistic attitude that God will bring them whatever is theirs without any kind of effort on their part. They believe that they do not need to be intentional about networking. Well, I have a message for those with that kind of attitude; planet Earth is run by people and God is not going to pour down your blessings from the sky, nor come down again from heaven to "bless" you. He is going to use people! People are his hands, feet and spokesmen. So, the more of the right kind of people that you are connected with, the more people God has at his disposal to use. It is not rocket science. When it comes to your outward connections with people, more is better. The more right kind of people that you know and who know you, the more vessels God has to use. The more people that can buy from you and support you, the more people that can speak for you and refer you and the more people you can influence and transform for the glory of God!

God designed us for relationships. We are created first for relationship with him and then for relationship with one another. Brian Hathaway estimated that forty four of the letters of the New Testament are about how we should get along with one another. This contrasts with about four percent on spiritual gifts. This emphasis is particularly clear when we look at the number of times the words "one another" occur, particularly in Paul's letters. The Greek word *allelon* occurs fifty-nine times as a specific command. That is the Biblical proof that the Master, Jesus, places huge emphasis on our relationships with one another and our relationships with one another greatly impacts our success. So, think twice before you burn that bridge with someone. Make sure you are not going to need it anytime soon!

Inward Connection

The third type of connection that is absolutely essential to your total success is your inward connection. Your inward connection speaks to how deeply and authentically connected you are to your divine purpose, passion, core values, and your unique personality and design. This connection will impact the following five factors that are critical to your personal, business and financial success:

Your Brilliance

Every individual walking this planet has been intentionally and uniquely designed to play a unique role in God's plan for humanity. His plan being that ultimately all of humanity will reign eternally with him in his Kingdom through repentance and faith in his Son. The unique role that we each have to play is as unique as our fingerprints and DNA. Your personality, talents, and experiences have been divinely bestowed upon you so that you have the ability to fulfill your unique role and purpose. When you function in your unique role, you function in your place of strength, and what some may refer to as your, "Zone of Brilliance." In this place, you are at your very best. Your performance is world class and success will come almost effortlessly and seamlessly. Someone once said when you are operating in your gift and talent, you have no competition. Proverbs 18:16 put it succinctly when it says that,

"A man's gift makes room for him and brings him before great men."

78

Your Income

There is a specific problem that faces humanity that only you can solve. You possess a unique talent that only you can OFFER to transform the world. It is a rare commodity and when you walk in it, the world will compensate you financially for it with millions of dollars. It is the simple law of supply and demand at work. You have a rare gift to solve a world-wide problem. Money is the consequence. Financial abundance is inevitable.

Your Happiness

Unfortunately, there are way too many people functioning outside their forte. They are busy trying to be like somebody else. They are trying to imitate someone else and because of that they are mediocre, unhappy and struggling at work and in life.

That actually used to be me a couple of years ago. I was involved in a relationship and part of a church community, that didn't fully recognize female apostolic leaders. I struggled with my identity, calling and gifts. I self-rejected. I felt like my personality and gifts were inconsistent with my gender and prayed and fasted to be like somebody else. I prayed not to be so assertive, outspoken, driven, bold and a visionary until one day I had an encounter with God that changed the trajectory of my life. In that encounter, God revealed to me that I did not make myself and that He was not mistaken when He made me female and equipped me with strong leadership abilities and personality. He made me understand that to self-reject was to reject his wisdom, purpose and plan. It was to say that somehow God didn't know what he was doing when He created me. It was to question and challenge his authority and wisdom!

Please know that you are neither an accident nor an after-thought! You were made on purpose and by design. It doesn't matter how you came into this world. It doesn't matter if you never knew your parents, whether your parents were married or not, or whether you were a product of an adulterous, incestuous or rape relationship. God foreknew you. He created you in love, for His unique purpose and equipped you with the unique gifts and talents that you need to fulfill your unique purpose.

Jeremiah 1 verse 5 says,

"I knew you before I formed you in your mother's womb. Before you were born I set you apart and appointed you as my prophet to the nations."

That means, you are predestined and preordained to be God's representation on the earth. His spokesperson to the nations of the world. It means you are predesigned and known by God. According to Psalm 139 verse 14, it means that you are *"fearfully and wonderfully made."*

It is time for you to look inwards, dig deep and discover you! It is time to discover your unique passion and gifts. It is time to tap into the hidden potential of what makes you uniquely you. And it is time for you to activate that gift and begin to walk in it.

When you begin to activate your gifts, then, and only then, will you begin to shine. You will begin to walk in your divine power and authority. This is the place where you will feel the most alive and awakened. It is the place where you will find tremendous joy and freedom and your youth will be renewed like that of an eagle.

Work will not seem like work. You will be walking on cloud 9 and getting paid lots of money to do you!

Your Calling

When you connect with who you intrinsically and innately are, you will be more readily able to find your place on the earth. You will be more readily able to attract your "tribe" and your "tribe" will be more readily able to locate you. The struggle will be over. You will show up fully present in the world and stand out as a beacon in the midst of the storm. You are not called to fit in, but to standout. You are not called to conform, but to transform. So, stop trying to fit in and belong. Step outside the box, standout and be uniquely you. You have a valuable and unique role to play in the kingdom.

Your Strength

Connecting inwardly with your inner passion and talent is like a fish in water. You are in your element. Fish don't learn how to swim; swimming is what they were created to do. Water is their natural habitat. Find your unique gifts and talent, function in it and watch yourself excel. You will become totally successful, because the place of our passion is the place of our strength. In that place you're not trying to be, you simply are. What you do comes naturally to you, and excellence and distinction will follow.

It is time for you to completely connect with who you are and who God made you to be intrinsically and authentically. Fully embrace your gifts and talents. Walk in your brilliance and shine your light in a very dark world. The whole of creation is waiting for you. Follow the admonishment of Isaiah 60: 1 -3,

"Arise, shine, for your light has come, and the glory of the LORD has risen upon you. 2 For behold, darkness shall cover the earth, and thick darkness the peoples; but the LORD will arise upon you, and his glory will be seen upon you. 3 And nations shall come to your light, and kings to the brightness of your rising."

When you are fully aligned and connected inwardly to your divine purpose and calling and walking in it, you will be sought-after, "kings will come to the brightness of your rising" and TOTAL success is inevitable.

CONCLUSION

When we examine the two greatest commands that Jesus gave us, they are concerned with our upward relationship with God, our inward relationship with loving ourselves and our outward relationship with one another (Matthew 22:36-40). Love God and love your neighbor as yourself. So much of the New Testament deals with relationships and connections. Jesus spent almost three years of his earthly ministry seeking and discipling a small group of followers into a true community.

Jesus, the Master, exemplified the power of the connection principle through His life and His messages. He was in right standing and lovingly connected upwardly with His Father, God, He was inwardly connected with His life's purpose and mission, and He was lovingly connected and in right standing with people. This is the reason why He was totally successful in his life's mission and purpose as the Savior of the world. His upward, inward and outward connections were properly aligned and formed a perfect right angle! The goal is to be like the Master and form a perfect right angle between the three types of connections.

Upward Connection

Inward Connection

Outward Connection

CHAPTER 11

MASTER-STRATEGY FOR ACCELERATED SUCCESS

I cannot talk about connections and fail to mention what I call the "golden-connection" for accelerated success. This "golden-connection" is none other than the mentor/mentee connection. After your upward connection with God, this is the most vital and absolutely the most critical connection to your success. It is so fundamental to your success that I have devoted a whole chapter to it. If you mean business about actualizing your God-given destiny and being totally successful at it, you must make this connection an integral part of your life.

The mentor/mentee connection is also referred to as a trainer/ trainee, coach/coachee, and a Disciple/Discipler relationship. This connection is absolutely crucial when it comes to making the connections that would propel you forward and cause you to advance at work and succeed in life.

Since the 1970s, mentoring has spread in the United States and is widely used by corporations and institutions, especially in training contexts. Odiorne, G. S. (1985) in "Mentoring – An American Management Innovation" *Personnel Administrator* (30): 63–65 described it as, "an innovation in American management.

The truth is that mentorship is not an American management "innovation" at all. It is a proven, ancient biblical strategy that existed since Bible times. The Bible is chock-full of examples of this winning work-life strategy:

Biblical Examples of Mentoring

- Moses and Joshua: Exodus 24: 13; 33: 11, Numbers 27: 20, Deuteronomy 34: 9, Numbers 11: 25
- Eli and Samuel: 1 Samuel 3: 1—4 & 22
- Saul and David: 1 Samuel 16: 23, 19: 9, 18: 18 & 23: 7
- Elijah and Elisha: 1 Kings 19: 19–21 & 2 Kings 2: 1-25
- Naomi and Ruth: Ruth 1: 16, Ruth 2: 17-18 & Ruth 3: 1-6
- Mordecai and Esther: Book of Esther
- Paul & Timothy : 2 Timothy 2: 17
- Elizabeth and Mary: Luke 1: 36
- Jesus and 12 Apostles: John 4: 8 & Luke 22: 8

In all the afore-mentioned Biblical examples, you will observe that the connection to a mentor was catalytic to the mentee actualizing their divine destiny and being totally successful. This is exactly how the connection with a spiritual or professional mentor works. They serve as a catalyst/propellant to your divine destiny. In the case of Ruth and Naomi, referenced in Chapter 9, the other daughter in law, Orpah, who severed her connection to Naomi, faded into oblivion – we never hear of her. The power of a mentor on the road to success cannot be over-emphasized.

What is Mentorship?

According to Wikipedia, the online encyclopedia,

"Mentorship is a personal developmental relationship in which a more experienced or more knowledgeable person helps to guide a less experienced or less knowledgeable person. The mentor may be older or younger, but have a certain area of expertise. It is a learning and development partnership between someone with vast experience and someone who wants to learn."

Mentoring is a process for the formal or informal transmission of knowledge, social capital, and the psychosocial support perceived by the recipient as relevant to work, career, or professional development. Mentoring entails formal or informal communication, during a sustained period of time, between a person who is perceived to have greater relevant knowledge, wisdom, or experience (the mentor), and a person who is perceived to have less (the protégé).

The Power of Mentorship

Mentoring is one of the fastest ways in overcoming obstacles and detours on the road to destiny and achieving total success. The benefits of having a mentor are invaluable and provide a lifeline in the sea of life that has far too many storms. Having a mentor can elevate your professional capabilities exponentially as you gain access to a wealth of knowledge, and real life practical experience. It can also help you accelerate your results as you save time by avoiding mistakes from trying to figure things out yourself.

Success is a specific destination and goal that you are trying to attain. It is a journey – a process. As with every journey, the road can be bumpy, detours and roadblocks will occur. No one in their sound mind will ever think of embarking on any kind of journey without a Global Positioning System (GPS) or a map. They realize that their journey is doomed for failure without these vital tools. Even if it is a road they have traveled on before, they feel more confident and self-assured with a GPS and/or map in hand.

That is exactly how having a mentor works. A mentor will provide you with six factors critical to your success. He or she will serve as your G.P.S. (Guide, Positioner and Support) and provide you with the road- M.A.P.* (Motivation, Accountability and Plan), as you travel on the road to destiny.

Below are the six key benefits, captured by the acronym GPS and MAP, of having this master-connection with a mentor:

G - Guidance

A good mentor is wise and willing to share his or her knowledge and experiences in order to help you succeed. It's like having a wonderful trusted ally ready to go whenever you're feeling unsure or in need of support. They can help you set and achieve career goals, make smart business decisions, overcome workplace challenges, learn new skills or simply offer an outside perspective when you're facing frustrations at work.

P – Positioner

Sometimes you struggle to find your place in life or at work. You struggle with your identity and divine calling. A mentor will help to steer you in the right direction of your goals and dreams. They provide the clarity you need to be positioned and aligned with your divine calling and destiny. A Biblical example is Eli and Samuel. The response that Eli asked Samuel to give to God, positioned Samuel for his prophetic ministry.

S – Support

A mentor will provide you with good emotional, mental and spiritual support. They can also connect you to a large pool of resources that will be pivotal to your success. Just knowing you are not alone is a huge sense of comfort and solace. Often the sense of isolation poses an obstacle to success.

M - Motivation

Mentees benefit from proactive encouragement from their mentors, who understand the power and value of this critical motivator. A biblical example is Barnabas and Paul in Acts 4:36-37; 9:26-30; 11:22-30. A mentor serves as a cheerleader of sorts. Cheering you on and providing motivation and encouragement as you journey to destiny. They often see what you don't see in yourself and with their encouragement, you will have confidence to go for your goals and dreams regardless of how big they are. When you are down, they are there to pick you up and keep you going.

A - Accountability

How many times have you set goals and not followed through? Or started out well with a particular goal or dream, but became distracted and veered off course? Having a mentor accountability partner is an invaluable benefit for asking tough questions, heading off danger, and derailing diversions. A Biblical example was Samuel and Saul in 1 Sam. 9-15. A mentor will help keep you on the straight and narrow. Someone once said that mentors are sometimes like "tor-mentors" because they hold you to a very high level of accountability and challenge you outside of your comfort zone! Having someone who can proffer concrete feedback and hold you accountable for your actions and decisions is a great anchor for your soul. There has to be someone in your life you respect enough to listen to, otherwise you will self-destruct.

P - Plan

A mentor will listen carefully to your passions, dreams, goals, hang-ups, and immature ideas and provide caring objective input and wisdom for you to actualize those goals and dreams. Many times your mentor has already traveled on the road you are traveling and they can provide you with a concrete plan and strategy to help you navigate and reach your destination faster. They provide valuable advice and objective input as personal and spiritual goals are thought through and established. Once established, mentors can then help to monitor, suggest adjustments, and counsel along the way as needed. A biblical example is Barnabas and John Mark; Acts 15:36-39; 2 Tim 4:11.

*Please refer to my eBook 'The Road-M.A.P. to Total Success' for more information about how Motivation, Accountability and a strategic Plan are the three top factors critical to your work-life success.

Conclusion

Mentoring relationships take various forms and can often be difficult to establish and navigate, but look for someone you can trust, someone with wisdom that has real life experiences and a proven track record of success. You don't get to choose all your other types of relationships, but you have control over who you chose to coach or mentor you. Choose wisely.

CHAPTER 12

'D.A.T.E.'™

TO MASTER YOUR CONNECTIONS

The idea behind a date is for two individuals to get to know one another better and explore their suitability to become more involved with one another, usually within a romantic context. The ultimate goal is to get to know each other better, find areas of shared interest, and build a mutually beneficial relationship based on mutual respect and understanding.

Even though Dates are often used more in the context of a romantic relationship, I believe that the idea behind dating has some key features that are fundamental to enhancing all the three essential types of connections that I have covered in this book; our upward, outward and inward connections. I personally have business "dates" and a "date night with God." My business dates are pre-scheduled, private times with a business associate or colleague. In the case of a "date night with God," it is a time of personal devotion and intimacy with God. I even schedule some "personal date time with myself!" Some call it, "me time." The idea is the same. Time spent alone, to get quiet with yourself, reflect, muse, catch up with reading or some other activity that you enjoy!

Using that context, I have created a unique technique and winning system and formula to help you master the art of building powerful and loyal connections that will accelerate your total success. This technique exposes the four main objectives behind a date by using the acronym of the word. My goal is to establish the four main features of a superb D.A.T.E., one that will help to deepen your connections and relationships and make you totally successful.

When scheduling a "D.A.T.E. with yourself," a "business D.A.T.E." and "D.A.T.E. night with God," be sure to keep the following four factors in mind. If you do, you will master the art and technique of building credible and profitable connections and relationships that will propel your personal, business and financial success.

D – Discovery

Think of dates as times of Discovery. A time of learning, sharing, fellowship and bonding. The goal is to bond and deepen the relationship, which is achieved by getting to know the other party better.

In Chapter 10, when talking about 'your connection and your influence,' I reference a very popular business adage that says, *"People do business with those they know, like and trust."* That means the MORE you KNOW, LIKE and TRUST someone, the STRONGER and deeper your connection will be with them, and the greater your ability to leverage that connection for your personal and professional advancement. So, schedule dates to spend quality time alone to listen to, and learn more about, your contacts and about God, as the case may be.

Discover God yourself by spending quality ALONE time with him. Discover what He likes, what He doesn't like and share some of your favorite things, your love language, your fears, and insecurities, and some of your deepest and innermost needs with Him.

It is a very good idea to take a **journal with you on your dates.** Write down what you learn about your date's values, passions, interests, goals, vision, etc. Listen to their heart.

Jesus exemplified this for us by spending quality time with His Father in prayer and quality time one on one with His disciples and He invites us in Matthew 11:28 to, *"learn from him."* We have to be intentional about knowing God by searching through the scriptures. We cannot know God outside of his word.

Many people make wrong decisions that negatively impact their success, jeopardize their health and finances simply because their zeal for God is not according to Biblical knowledge. For example, someone recently reached out to me and said God told her to marry this serial criminal who is abusive towards her and steals from her! Well, it only took me a second to know she did not hear from God because the "revelation" does not line up with the word of God. God says in 2 Corinthians 6:16 that we should not be "unequally yoked," how can that same God then ask you to yoke unequally with a criminal?!

To avoid that kind of mistake, it is crucial that you schedule meaningful time alone to get to study God's word for yourself and get to know Him better. You will get a greater appreciation of His heart, His voice, His values, and His character, and be better able to align yours with His. In doing so, you will be positioned for His blessings and total success will be yours.

Even in your personal and professional relationships, scheduling this time of discovery will save you a lot of pain and heartache. You will avoid or catch incompatible relationships early and build stronger compatible relationships from practicing this simple technique of discovery. One of the key factors to look out for during your discovery date is making sure that you both share the same values and vision. Connecting with someone who doesn't share the same values and vision will cause you to run into serious problems. Even in your business connections, make sure you are all on the same page about the things that really matter to you.

Bear in mind, that the goal is for you to get to know each other better and communication is a two way street. Don't be the only one sharing. It is important to listen to the other party, whether that is God, your customers, clients, boss, and other business associates. Do YOU wait to listen?

A – Appreciation

Everyone likes to feel loved and valued, and that includes God! When people feel loved and valued, they go beyond the call of duty. They bend over backwards to support and accommodate – they give of themselves! That is why your D.A.T.E. times must include this powerful motivational factor called appreciation. It is a winning technique for building loyal, loving and supportive relationships. Never go on a date empty handed. Always go with a gift to express your gratitude. It doesn't have to be anything fancy or expensive. It could be a promotional product for a client, a card, flowers, chocolates for a friend. The goal is to demonstrate gratitude, appreciation, love and respect. You have to be intentional about including this technique if you mean business about building profitable connections.

Since we don't see God face to face and cannot buy him a gift, when it comes to your date night with God, you express your gratitude verbally through worship and prayers of thanksgiving. Jesus laid this example down for us in the Lord's Prayer when he admonished us to begin our prayers by "hallowing" the name of God.

Psalm 100:4, invites us to, *"enter into his gates with thanksgiving, and into his courts with praise: be thankful unto him, and bless his name."*

You should always begin your date night with God with WORSHIP, GRATITUDE and REVERENCE. One good habit is to write at least ten things you are thankful for in your journal every week, and go through them individually, expressing gratitude to God for them during your date. You can also express gratitude to God by giving a donation and/or buying a gift for a ministry, and/or spiritual leader.

Appreciation is a powerful motivating factor that serves to deepen connections and helps to open your spirit for a greater in-flow of blessings. In the Parable of The Ten Lepers that Jesus shared in Luke 17: 11-19, the leper that came back got a bigger blessing as he was made whole. The other nine simply got healed.

The idea of appreciating God and appreciating others is also applicable to "dates" you schedule with yourself! Include time to appreciate yourself. This comes by way of celebrating your successes no matter how small. Stop beating yourself up so much. Take time to treat yourself, indulge yourself, buy a gift for yourself and give yourself a pat on the shoulder. You may not be where you want to be, but you are definitely not where you used to be. Take time to de-stress, relax, laugh, smile and unwind. It will keep you fresh, keep your creative juices flowing and keep you on the cutting edge. That is the way to stay ahead of your competitors and be totally successful.

Include appreciation in all your D.A.T.E.s, and watch both your upward, outward and inward connections skyrocket.

T – Time Alone

One of the key factors in strengthening any type of relationship is to invest quality time alone with yourself or your date. Three they say is a crowd. The deepest form of intimacy is carried out in private between two individuals. This is the time when people are most vulnerable and most authentic. When others are around, you might find it harder for people to open up to you. That is why time alone is critical to building strong relationships.

By time alone, I mean pre-scheduled, undistracted and uninterrupted time that is primarily devoted to that individual for the sole purpose of getting to know them better. It is the highest kind of honor and respect that you can show a person when you clear your schedule, and give them your time and full attention in private. And, like I said in the previous section, people respond very well to feeling valued and respected when you bend over backwards to accommodate them. There is also nothing that can damage a connection more than being distracted during a date or allowing other programs to take up the time you schedule for your date. So, it is pivotal as you schedule your "D.A.T.E.s" that you think time – quality time. Think quality, not necessarily quantity. Based on Matthew 26: 40, where Jesus asked his disciples, *"Couldn't you men keep watch with me for one hour?"*

I usually set one hour as the minimum time to spend with God on a "date night."

To me quality also means a secluded, private location and undivided attention with no interruptions including answering phones, texting and being on social media!

E – Enjoyment

The fourth feature of a D.A.T.E. that deepens connections is enjoyment. Dates ought to be fun and relaxed. Some of the biggest business deals have been made on a golf course or at some social after business hours event. Actually, you learn more about who people truly are when they are in more relaxed and social environments. Include laughter and entertainment on your dates. When it is with God laughter can take the form of some nice praise and worship music. Dance, sing, and be merry in His presence. With professional and/or personal connections, you can also include music, a comedian and other types of fun activities. There are several social business- after-hour networking events that you can invite a business associate to, so you can bond and get to know them better. For me, I produce a quarterly social event known as "An Evening of Inspired Success." It is highly-acclaimed and one of my proven marketing strategies to strengthen my connections with my clients and prospects.

I challenge you to start to apply this D.A.T.E. technique to your upward, outward and inward connections, and watch your connections and influence deepen as you are rewarded with a loyal following who will gladly support you and joyfully invest in you!

AFFIRMATION: I affirm and boldly declare that I am a consummate and dynamic networker. I know the value of connections and I am intentional about deepening my upward connection with God, my outward connection with people, and my inward connection with myself. I will schedule quality time and invest generously in cultivating these three essential connections. And because I am intentional about strengthening these relationships, I declare that I am in a loving relationship with God, with myself and with others. Subsequently, I am blessed with people who know, like and trust me and are willing to help support and refer me. I benefit from a lot of good will and information that accelerates my professional, personal and spiritual success. I automatically attract only positive people in my life. I am intuitive and my steps are ordered by the Lord, so I connect with mentors and coaches who provide me with the guidance and wisdom that propels me forward. I am not slack concerning my personal time of devotion with God. God takes priority in my life and my connection with him is sound and Biblically based. I am like Jesus, I don't have a cubicle mentality. I step outside my comfort zone and declare that regardless of my personality, I am bold about stepping outside my geographical, racial and denominational lines to build relationships.

CHAPTER 13

THE COMMUNICATION PRINCIPLE

"If the trumpet does not sound a clear call, who will get ready for battle?!" – 1 Corinthians 14 verse 8

"Power of life and death is in the tongue." – Proverbs 18 verse 21

Communication is the third top proven foundational principle for actualizing your goals and dreams and achieving personal, professional and financial success. It is critical therefore that in your journey to total success that you MASTER your communication, and make sure that it is carefully crafted and targeted to elicit a positive response from your message. This is because the actions and behavior that you will elicit from people is governed by your communication. Your communication determines how people respond to you. Whether they will hire you for a job, vote for you, buy a product or service from you, buy into your dream or vision, donate into your ministry, agree to marry you and all other personal, professional or spiritual goals and dreams that you may have, rests squarely on your communication. To master the art of communication is to master the art of persuading and influencing people to take positive action and actions favorable to you. It is also to master one of the foundational pillars of success. Failure to master this critical foundational principle of success means that you will not elicit actions and behavior from people that will propel you forward, which ultimately means you will be stuck at your current level of success and not experience growth.

What is Communication

According to the Encarta English Dictionary, communication is:

"The exchange of information between people, e.g. by means of speaking, writing, speaking signs or using a common system of signs of behavior."

I define communication as the dissemination of information to an individual and/or group of people through word, writing, action, video or sign language. It is the process involving the exchange of information, thoughts, ideas and emotions between a sender and receiver. The sender encodes and sends the message, via the communication channel, to the receiver who decodes the message.

There are different types of communication. Communication can be:

- Verbal

- Non-Verbal (Body language, Dress, etc.)

- Written

- Visual (Filmic)

- Graphic

There are also different mediums of communication:

Video (Television)

Audio (Radio, Music, Podcasts)

Print (Emails, Books, Newspapers, Articles, Blogs etc.)

Physical (Dance, Acting, Plays and Drama)

THE POWER OF COMMUNICATION

Humans act only in response to messages. We are like computers that are "programmed" to behave in a certain way. Without the input of information and "programming," we simply are incapable of any kind of ACTION. Messages inform, educate and instruct. In other words, messages are to humans what gasoline is to a vehicle. It is what gets us moving and going!

You are constantly sending messages and communicating, every second and every minute of the day; messages to yourself, through your thoughts, words and deeds, and messages to others through the same mediums. Every message you send elicits some type of response – a response that is either favorable or unfavorable to you.

There are two main factors that will impact your communication:

Your Influence

As I said earlier, communication impacts your ability to persuade and influence people. It can be positive or negative. Whether people are going to do business with you is determined by your communication. For your communication to influence people positively, it must be clear, concise, authentic, and persuasive, and must have a call to action. You must have an end in mind. Ask yourself this question, what is the response that I am trying to elicit from my listener?   Carefully craft your message accordingly.

The connection between communication and success is not readily apparent or obvious. It is one of those hidden factors. As a result, people often speak without giving much thought to their words and actions, not realizing that every bit of communication is influencing how people perceive them and their decisions to determine if they want to be in any kind of relationship with them; personally, professionally, or spiritually.

The key to successful communication is to be intentional and pay close attention to your communication. Bear in mind that communication is not only verbal, it is written, it is visual, it is graphic, it is physical! Especially in this virtual social world that we live in, make sure that your posts, pictures, videos, profiles, websites, etc. are consistent with your brand and the opinion you want people to have about you. ALL of your communication is influencing people in one way or another.

Many have been denied opportunities and even fired from their jobs because of something they shared socially. Pay attention to your tone of voice and body language as well, as these also go a long way in influencing people and ultimately impacts your success. The gestures you make, the way you sit, how fast or how loud you talk, how close you stand, how much eye contact you make; these all send strong messages. The way you look can communicate interest, affection, hostility or attraction. Eye contact is also important in maintaining the flow of conversation and for gauging the other person's response. All these are hidden factors that are impacting your ability to influence people.

Your Results

Like I stated earlier, your communication impacts the response that you get from people, as far as them buying from you or hiring you. Which means ultimately your results and success will be determined by your communication. We are all in the sales business; selling one thing or the other. Even our spiritual calling and destiny is about sales - we are salesmen of Jesus! We are trying to "sell" Jesus to a dying world. How many deals will you close and how many sales will you make? Your results and your success depends on your communication. Your communication must connect with people; it must speak directly to their pain and need. It must be credible and convincing before they can buy from you.

Bear in mind that people respond better to kindness than harshness. Proverbs says 1: 1 says, *"A soft answer turns away wrath."*

So keep your communication positive and inspiring. Compliment people. Express belief in abilities, talents and skills. Let them know you are available and that you are rooting for them. Use words like "Yes, YOU can-do it!" Remember the golden rule, even when you have to speak the truth, make sure you do it in love. Be pleasant and polite, just as Ephesians 4:15 admonishes us. Communicating in this manner will make you more loved and will enhance your results.

The power of communication cannot be over-emphasized. Communication is the foundation of successful relationships. When done effectively, it enhances people's sense of value and worth, increases contentment and satisfaction, prevents resentment, conflict and violence and boosts morale, performance, productivity and loyalty. It will increase the buy-in into your vision and dreams and ultimately, your success.

CHAPTER 14

THE FIVE ESSENTIAL C'S OF COMMUNICATION

There are 5 essential factors that will elevate the quality and effectiveness of your communication to the level where people are willing and excited to support and remain loyal to you. The five essentials of effective and results driven communication are:

Clarity

Sending confusing and mixed messages is the number one killer of communication. Make sure your communication is clear of any ambiguity. Get clear about who you are, what your purpose is, how you want to accomplish your purpose and mission and who you are called to serve. Jesus modeled this for us and I believe that this was one of the key factors responsible for His success. There was NO one whose identity was challenged as much as Jesus, and NO one who was extremely clear, specific and emphatic about their identity and mission as Jesus!

There are several verses in the gospel of John where Jesus clearly articulated his identity. He made over twenty "I am" statements to clearly communicate his identity. For example, in John 6:51, he says:

*"**I am** the living bread which came down from heaven."*

In John 8:23, he says:

*"And He said to them, you are from beneath; **I AM from above**. You are of this world; I am not of this world."*

John 8:12:

*Then Jesus spoke to them again, saying, "**I AM the light of the world**. He who follows me shall not walk in darkness, but have the light of life."*

He was also very clear about his mission. In John 10:10 he said,

*"I am come **that they might have life**, and that they might have it more abundantly."*

In Mark 2:17 he says,

*"I came not to **call** the righteous, but **sinners to repentance**." And in Luke 19:10, "For the Son of man is **come to seek and to save that which was lost**."*

Lastly, Jesus was very clear about His timing. Jesus said to His mother at the Wedding at Canaan in **John 2:4;** *"Woman, what concern is that to you and to me? My hour has not yet come."*

Jesus, to the Jews: **John 7:6 & 8** – Jesus said to them, "My time has not yet come, but your time is always here." John 7:8 – "Go to the festival yourselves. I am not going to this festival, for my time has not yet fully come."

Jesus to his Disciples Announcing His Departure: **Matthew 20 v 18:**

His clarity in these three areas allowed him to communicate effectively and people responded to his message. Don't be afraid of clearly communicating your:

- Mission: The purpose for which you and/or your organization exits

- Objective: The results you are trying to accomplish

- Values: What you stand for and believe in

- Expectations: What you are seeking to accomplish through your message

- Boundaries: The lines in which people can operate

- Time-limits: your deadlines and turn-around periods

Concise

Keep your communication short and sweet. In this day of information overload, less is definitely more when it comes to communication. The shorter it is, the more memorable it is. I am sure you can remember of 2-3 sentences from jingles you heard in commercials from a long time ago, because the lines were short and catchy.

Cogent

The more forceful and persuasive your communication, the more effective it will be. People are emotional and research has proven that more people tend to respond emotionally. It is about how they feel. So, add some power and emotion to your communication and you will, more than likely, elicit positive responses from them. It also makes you and your message more relatable.

Credible

Always speak the truth and be authentic. As stated previously, 'People do business with those they know, like and trust.' Trust is easy to break and hard to build. Honesty is the best policy. Part of being credible is being authentic. No pretense, no bull, keep it real!

Call to Action

The fifth essential factor of an effective results driven communication is that it must possess a call to action. Remember, there should be an end to which communication is directed. Always drive your listeners to take that action. Whether it is telling others to repent of their sins and accept Jesus as their Lord and Savior, buying a product from you, hiring you for a job, giving you a raise or accepting your bid for a contract, always make the call. Always end with a call to action. Effective communication must always motivate and inspire people to action. Without it, you will not close deals and you wouldn't be totally successful. Don't be afraid to make the call.

CHAPTER 15

'T. A. L. K.'™

TO MASTER YOUR COMMUNICATION

Even though I believe that there are some gifted communicators born with the innate ability to communicate powerfully and effectively, I also believe that communication is an art that anyone can master, and must master if they want to be totally successfully at work and in life. Whether it is to persuade someone to hire you for a job, negotiate for a promotion, convince someone to vote or buy from you or to close a deal in the boardroom, there is an increasing need to master the art of persuasive presentations and pitches. In addition to the foregoing, the globalization of the world and the advent of social media and the internet has also made it imperative to master this vital success principle because we are "talking" to people more often now, than ever before. It behooves you, therefore, to make sure that you are "talking" effectively so that your voice can be heard, and people can respond to your message in the manner that you desire.

The good news is that it is possible to master the art of communication and "T.A.L.K." your way to success! There are four critical factors that govern the revolutionary system that I have created to help you "T.A.L.K." your way to success. If you pay close attention to these four factors, you will conquer any fear of speaking you may have and take your communication to another level. The four factors are:

T – Target

The first step in mastering the art of effective communication is to target your message. You must absolutely be clear about who your message is for – who your target audience is. You must do extensive research and get to the nitty gritty about their demographics. Ask yourself such questions like:

1. Who are they?
2. What is their age?
3. What is the level of their education?
4. What is their race?
5. What is their profession?
6. What is their spiritual/religious background?
7. What are their shopping habits?
8. What is their gender?
9. What is their political affiliation?
10. What is their income?

The reason why this is such a crucial first step in mastering the art of effective and results driven communication is that the clearer you are about your target audience, the more targeted you can make your message, and the more you can speak the language of your audience. Bear in mind that the tone of voice, your dress style, marketing materials, choice of colors and words are all factors that you weave in to target your message appropriately. For example, you would speak differently to a group of white collar professionals than you would to a group of blue collar workers. You speak differently to middle schoolers than you would to college students. And you would speak differently to a black male audience than you would to a white male audience! This is because people have different learning styles and cultural verbiage based on their background, race, age, gender, education, etc. The more your listeners can resonate with your message, the higher your chances of getting them to buy into your message. The goal is for your message to connect and resonate with your listeners within sixty seconds or less, or else you run the risk of losing their attention and losing it forever! People have a very short attention span.

A - Articulate Value (What's In It For Them)

It's about them, it's not about you! Everyone listening to you is asking themselves this question, "What is in it for me (WIFM)?!" So, effective and results driven communication must always articulate the value that you deliver to your audience. It is not about showing off or demonstrating how brilliant you are to your audience. So, don't focus on yourself, but focus on your audience and articulate the value and benefit that they will derive from listening to you, buying your product and/or hiring you for a job, whatever the case may be. This is often called the "Unique Selling Proposition." One of the biggest mistakes that I see people make is focusing on the product and their process, not the unique transformational value that the people derive from investing in them and/or their product or services. The second step in the T.A.L.K. technique is to learn how to speak to their pain and articulate value. At this point, you also want to articulate your call to action. What is the response you want or the action you want them to take? Make sure that it is clearly articulated as well.

L - Listen (Non Verbal Cues)

True communication is a two way street. It is just as important for you to listen as it is for you to talk. Great communicators are also great listeners. There are different ways of listening to people. Interviews, focus groups, surveys, evaluations, assessment reports, comments and suggestions. Those are some of the few ways that you can listen to your audience to get the constructive feedback that will help you improve and grow. In an in-person or visual communication, pay attention to non-verbal or non-written cues. Sadly, I see too many people who get offended and take the feedback personally and stay stuck in their comfort zone. Don't take it personally, listen to your audience. Even though it might be difficult to do, try and listen to people even when the feedback is not delivered in the most positive manner. In such cases, the goal for you is to separate the emotion from the facts and endeavor to listen to the essence of the message. In that negative criticism, you will find some truth that can help you build upon your success and grow.

The fastest way to lose loyalty and credibility is to refuse to listen to your audience. They will eventually speak with their money or their feet, because they will feel disrespected and unvalued. Master the art of listening and you will have mastered a critical factor in effective communication.

Of course if you are the individual offering feedback, you must strive to, as the Bible says, "speak the truth in love." Communication is not just what you say, but *how* you say it. There is a direct relationship between the way a message is delivered and the way it is received. If you want others to consider your critique and feedback, then it must be delivered effectively.

K - Keep Practicing

No matter how proficient you are at speaking, practice they say makes perfect. Take up any chances you have to speak and present. Even though some have claimed it is a myth, I still believe that it takes several thousands of hours, if not the ten thousand that was touted in the book *Outliers* by Malcolm Gladwell, to master a skill, grow in your confidence and become a recognized expert that commands great income and influence. So keep practicing. Keep on keeping on. Practicing helps you learn from your mistakes, tweak your strategy, and improve on your performance.

Conclusion

Jesus was very masterful at using this technique. He always targeted his messages using verbiage and analogies that His audience could relate to. He articulated the value He delivered, offering eternal life and a place in His Father's kingdom as His, "unique selling proposition." He listened to his followers and responded to their critique appropriately, and He never stopped speaking. He looked for any avenue and means to get his message out. He spoke from books, in desert places, on mountains, in synagogues - He kept on until the very end and was extremely skillful in His communication using the right nuances, pauses and non-verbal cues to drive home the message.

The art of effective and persuasive presentations can be summarized in S.M.A.R.T. Be S.M.A.R.T. with your communication.

That is be,

S - Simplistic "Broadly speaking, the short words are the best, and the old words best of all" says Winston Churchill

M - Memorable by K.I.S.S. (Keep It Short and Sweet)

A - Affirming: validate your listeners

R - Reverential: include the 3P's: Politeness, Pleasantries, Poised (leveled tone of voice and body language)

T - Teach: instructive, call to action and deliver value

AFFIRMATION: I declare and decree that I am a masterful and dynamic communicator. I am very clear about my life's mission, vision, audience and my unique selling proposition. I articulate it clearly, concisely and boldly whenever I need to. I am not afraid to make the call, nor call people to action. I am mindful and cognizant of the power of communication. I skillfully and intentionally communicate in ways that build people up and not tear people down. No idle words will come out of my mouth because I am snared by the words of my mouth, and I will eat the fruit of my lips. I always speak the truth and I do it in love. I speak in such a way that I dispel conflict not incite one. Everything about me communicates consistently who I am, what I represent and what I stand for. So I dress right, post the right pictures and all of my other marketing materials are carefully crafted to speak to my brand and communicate my excellence, integrity and credibility.

MEET THE MASTER

"And they lifted up their voices, and said, Jesus, Master, have mercy on us." – Luke 17:13

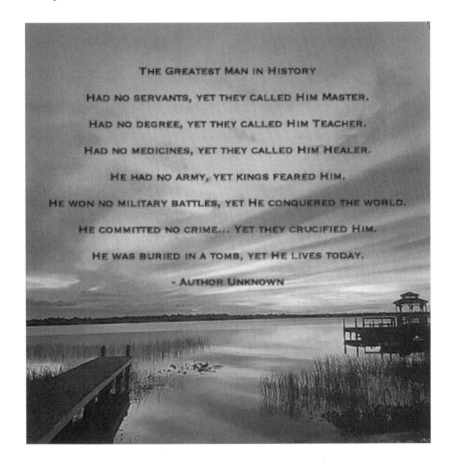

THE GREATEST MAN IN HISTORY

HAD NO SERVANTS, YET THEY CALLED HIM MASTER.

HAD NO DEGREE, YET THEY CALLED HIM TEACHER.

HAD NO MEDICINES, YET THEY CALLED HIM HEALER.

HE HAD NO ARMY, YET KINGS FEARED HIM.

HE WON NO MILITARY BATTLES, YET HE CONQUERED THE WORLD.

HE COMMITTED NO CRIME... YET THEY CRUCIFIED HIM.

HE WAS BURIED IN A TOMB, YET HE LIVES TODAY.

- AUTHOR UNKNOWN

A FEW FACTS ABOUT HIM

His Identity - Jesus Christ of Nazareth, the Son of the Living God – John 6: 69 & Mark 1: 1, 24 & 39

His Name: - Immanuel (eem-mah-noo-EL) God with us - Matthew 1:23 & Isaiah 7: 14

His Position: The 2nd Person of the Trinity… the word that was in the beginning that became flesh – Matthew 28: 19, John 1: 1-5 & Timothy 3:16

His Mission: To reconcile man back to an intimate loving relationship with a Holy and righteous God by paying the penalty of their sins and removing the middle wall of partition that separated them through his death on the cross - Mark 2:17, Luke 19: 10 & Ephesians 2:14

His Vision: For men to escape the eternal damnation of hell and reign forever with Him in His Kingdom – John 3: 5

HOW TO HAVE

A RELATIONSHIP WITH HIM

- **A**dmit you're a sinner – "For all have sinned and come short of the glory of God." – Romans 3:16

- **B**elieve on the Lord Jesus Christ – "Believe on the Lord Jesus Christ, and thou shalt be saved." - Acts 16: 31

- **C**onfess – Confess and repent of your sins – "And with the mouth confession is made unto salvation." – Romans 9:10

- **D-** Decide for and commit to your life to him – "Present yourself a living sacrifice." – Romans 12:1

PRAYER FOR SALVATION

Dear Jesus,

I come to you today admitting that I am a sinner who has sinned against you in my thoughts, words and deeds. I believe that you're God's Son who came to die for me on the cross. I repent and confess my sins and ask that you forgive me of all my sins. I decide and give my life to you today and ask that you come into my heart. I receive you as my Lord and personal Savior. Write my name in the Book of Life. Give me the strength and grace to live for you from this day forward. In Jesus' mighty name, I pray.

Dated, this _____ (day) of _____
(month) _____ (year)

If you prayed that prayer and meant it, congratulations, you are now saved! Welcome to the family of God!

Now that you are saved

Read your Bible and pray every day if you want to grow. For group fellowship and support, you are welcome to join Princess Bola @ The Gathering Place Online for live, virtual prayer and Bible study on Sundays at 1pm EST. Learn more at: www.RoyalProclamations.com

ABOUT THE AUTHOR

As America's *"Dream-midwife, Spiritual Money Coach and Queen of Networking,"* Princess Bola Adelani, aka the Total Success Coach, equips people to master the four pillars of TOTAL success; money, mind, people, and spirit so that they can exponentially grow their influence and deepen their impact in the marketplace. Her ultimate goal is to provide them with the "POWER" and proven practical strategies to fulfill their higher calling as transformers and leaders of change and to serve as a catalyst for them to unlock their **P**assions, seize **O**pportunities, gain **W**isdom, build on their **E**xperience and get **R**esults™. It is her formula for TOTAL success!

She is the Founder and CEO of <u>Royal Proclamations</u>; a personal and professional training firm based in Hartford, Connecticut, which inspires thousands globally to greater personal and professional fulfillment. She is also lead Pastor and Apostle at, <u>The Gathering Place</u>; a fresh and revolutionary virtual NU (New & Unique) Church movement.

Princess Bola is an internationally recognized work-life expert and the recipient of several awards, including the 2008 Microsoft sponsored Connecticut Small Business and Minority Elevator Pitch Award. She has been featured in several national and international magazines, and radio and television networks including: Fox CT, LA Talk Radio, WIHS Radio, Beautifully Inspired Women's magazine and Women Empowering Women magazine (a UK based publication).

A dynamic, bold and powerful speaker, a revolutionary thought leader and a masterful business strategist, Princess Bola speaks globally in a variety of settings and mentors several individuals on their business and life issues.

She is a British-trained corporate lawyer with an honors law degree from England's University of Buckingham and she has also obtained a certificate in Women's Leadership in Applied Spirituality from Hartford Seminary.

Princess Bola is the proud mom of two teenage boys, Emmanuel and Enoch, who she fondly refers to as her "two young lions."

People often ask Bola if she is a real princess. Indeed, she is an authentic and true princess. Her paternal grandfather was crown-prince of Owu-Ikija, Ijebu tribe, in Nigeria's Southwestern state of Ogun and her uncle, her father's immediate younger brother, is the current king of the town. More important to her, however, is the royal heritage she shares with millions of others as a daughter of Jesus Christ, the King of Kings!

More information on Princess Bola is available at: www.RoyalProclamations.com

.

Made in the USA
San Bernardino, CA
27 December 2019